Diary of a Confederate Sharpshooter

The Life of James Conrad Peters

Edited and Annotated by:
Jack L. Dickinson

*Best wishes,
Jack
Dickinson*

Pictorial Histories Publishing Co., Inc.
Charleston, West Virginia 25301

LIBRARY OF CONGRESS
CATALOG CARD
NUMBER 97-69569

ISBN 1-57510-033-9

First Printing: December 1997

Cover Art: Jeffrey A. Dickinson

PICTORIAL HISTORIES PUBLISHING CO., INC.
1416 Quarrier Street, Charleston, West Virginia 25301

James Conrad Peters
B: Jan. 25, 1840
D: Jan. 9, 1911
Pvt., French's Battery Va. Light Artillery (1861-62)
Sgt., 30th Battalion Va. Sharpshooters (1862-65)

Camp Douglas,

A Union prison camp for Confederate soldiers near Chicago, Illinois:

> *"March 16th 1862 Have got about well I think.*
>
> *Thank God for it for it is bad to be sick here."*

James C. Peters

Table of Contents

Acknowledgments

I wish to extend sincere thanks to several people who assisted with this work. Thanks certainly go to Mr. Henry Anderson of Mullens, West Virginia for the loan of the original Peters diary. Mr. Anderson also acted as our guide on a hike to the site of Mercer Salt Works on a beautiful fall day. Special thanks go to my wife Kay, who acted as my first editor. Without her help, patience, and support I would never have been able to bring anything to publication. Our son, Ted Dickinson, also assisted with editing. Mr. Gordon Cotton, Director of the Old Court House Museum and Davis Memorial in Vicksburg deserves special thanks for all the great information he provided on Vicksburg and the boats on the Mississippi River. Also thanks to the folks at the West Virginia Dept. of Culture and History (West Virginia Archives) and the helpful folks at the Alderman Library at the University of Virginia. The people at the Huntington office, U.S. Army Corps of Engineers were helpful in pinpointing the cemeteries that were relocated during the Bluestone Dam project, and provided maps showing the grave locations. Thanks also to Rob Smith at Point Lookout, Maryland State Park for his help on the Point Lookout prison camp.

Jack L. Dickinson

Preface

This is the story of James Conrad Peters, with emphasis on the five year period recounted in his diary or journal. The diary spans the five year period from September 1858 to February 1863. The diary is important for two reasons. First, it gives us insight into the man himself. He wrote poems, music, lists, and day-by-day accounts of his Civil War service in the Confederate Army. Secondly, it gives us a rare account of prison life in a Union POW camp. It is a small, leather-covered, pocket notebook with a leather flap. The diary entries were mainly recorded in soft pencil and many entries are faint. The first part of the diary contains a running commentary of Peters' travels during the summer of 1859, when he observed and inspected various tracts of land in the rugged New River and Kanawha River Valleys of present-day West Virginia. He began his Civil War account on Sept. 25, 1861 and his last dated entry was Feb. 3, 1863. The diary has remained in possession of the immediate family since the War. In the 1940's it was in the possession of one of James C. Peters' daughters, Annie Laura (Mrs. J. G. Anderson.) At that time she lived at Athens, Mercer Co., West Virginia. It is now in the possession of her grandson, Mr. Henry Anderson of Mullens, West Virginia. We are grateful to Mr. Anderson for the loan of the diary.

This annotated biography of the life of James Conrad Peters also by necessity becomes an account of the two Confederate units to which he belonged. First was Napoleon B. French's Battery Virginia Light Artillery (or simply French's Battery.) Later this unit was reorganized into the 30th Battalion Virginia Sharpshooters (infantry.) Therefore some setting straight of the record is in order. Through many records, even including records and maps from the Ft. Donelson National Battlefield Park, the Confederate artillery battery to which James Conrad Peters belonged and which fought at Ft. Donelson is referred to as D. A. French's Battery. This is obviously incorrect. Peters' diary and other historical evidence (such as the Compiled Service Records) point out conclusively that the battery was Napoleon B. French's Battery. Probably the original unit, before its conversion to artillery, was known as Napoleon B. French's Company of Virginia Volunteers. Notations in the Compiled Service Records of the later organization (30th Battalion Virginia Sharpshooters) mention the historically correct designation of the artillery unit as Capt. Napoleon B. French's Battery Virginia Light Artillery. There was indeed another company commanded by D.A. French, a distant relative of Napoleon French. It was designated David A. French's Giles County Artillery. This company, however, was near Elizabeth City, North Carolina during the Battle of Fort Donelson. This error occurred due to a statement in Gen. Bushrod Johnson's report of the battle dated March 4, 1862, in which he mistakenly referred to the Virginia unit at Ft. Donelson as being commanded by Capt. D. A. French.

James Conrad Peters had a unique military career in the Confederate Army. He served in the cavalry, artillery and infantry without ever transferring from his original unit! Upon his enlistment, his Virginia Volunteer unit was designated as cavalry, but within a few months it was changed to artillery and allocated four cannon. After the unit's capture at Ft. Donelson along with their cannon, the unit was reorganized as a sharpshooter battalion of infantry. James' experiences through the War and his survival through two of the most horrible Union prison camps provide a lesson in courage, faith and perseverance. His unshakable faith in God and his love of family makes his story fascinating.

Photos of the Peters Diary.

Chapter I
Ancestors

We begin our account of the life and times of James Conrad Peters with a look back at his ancestors. All of us who are descended from James should indeed be proud of our heritage, not only because we are descended from a Revolutionary War soldier, but also because of the military tradition that continued in this family through the War of 1812, the Civil War, and into the 20th century.

James's great grandfather was Christian Peters who was born Oct. 16, 1760 in Rockingham County, Virginia. According to his pension application, he served as a private with Capt. Robert Craven's Company and was engaged in battles with the Indians. He reenlisted in Sept., 1780 and served six months as corporal again in Capt. Craven's Company and was in the battles at Georgetown and Cowpens. He enlisted again in 1781 and served as sergeant in Capt. Jeremiah Beasley's Company and Col. Jack Willis' Virginia Regiment and was in the battles of Hotwater and Jamestown.[1] This service in the Revolution granted Christian Peters land, and he and his brother John (who was also a Revolutionary War veteran) moved from Rockingham County to the New River Valley in present-day Monroe County, West Virginia after the end of Christian's military service. This was probably about 1794. Christian married Anna Katherine Fudge on May 3, 1785. She was the daughter of John Fudge who came to America from Germany in 1744. Christian and Anna Katherine had eight children that are documented. They are: Conrad Lewis, born March 14, 1786; John, born Feb. 27, 1788; Jacob, born Jan. 8, 1791; Mary (or Molly) born May 20, 1793; Elizabeth, born June 15, 1795; Rhoda, born Aug. 3, 1798; Nancy, born Sept. 4, 1801; and Sarah (or Sallie) born June 14, 1804.[2]

Christian Peters donated the land for the town that now bears his name: Peterstown, Monroe County, West Virginia. It was said of him: "He was a man of energy and push and to him must be credited, among his various enterprises, the building of the first grist mills in the community..."[3] Christian died on Oct. 18, 1837 and is buried in the Peterstown Cemetery where his grave is marked with a Revolutionary War marker.

Christian's son, Conrad Lewis Peters, was born at Peterstown. Conrad was a blacksmith and tavern-keeper, owning a tavern near Peterstown. He was also a major in the 108th Virginia Militia during the War of 1812. This regiment was formed at Union, the county seat of Monroe County, and supposedly was packed and ready to go to war when peace was declared in 1815.[4] Conrad also grew tobacco on a large plantation. He was a member of the County Court and a Justice of the Peace of Monroe County. In 1825 he was appointed Sheriff and was authorized to select deputies. Conrad Lewis married Clara Snidow on July 20, 1809 in Giles County, Virginia. Conrad and Clara had at least 13 children. Their second child, Christian Snidow Peters, who was born July 1, 1812 would become the father of our subject, James Conrad Peters.

Christian Snidow Peters married Mary Elizabeth Karnes at Peterstown on March 10, 1835. Like his father Christian Snidow was a blacksmith and manager of a plantation. The census of 1850 locates Christian Snidow Peters and his family in Monroe County, and his occupation is shown as blacksmith. His son, James Conrad, is shown as being eleven years old.[5] Supposedly after most of his children were born he moved

Peters Family
Ancestor Chart

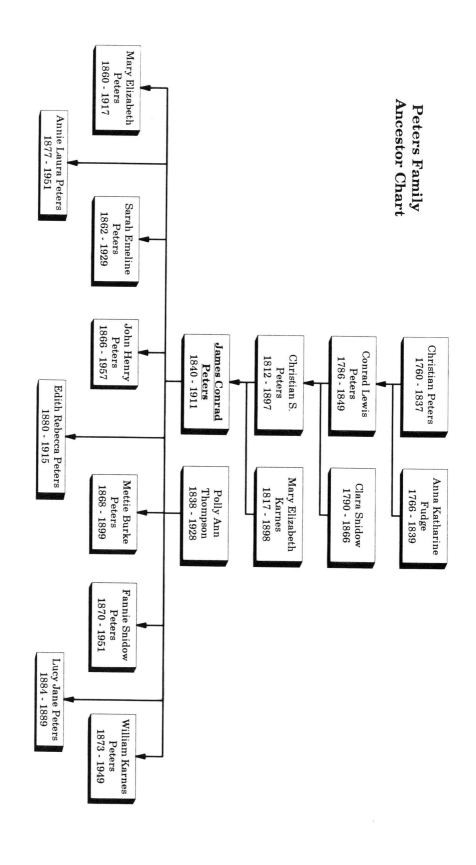

Mary Elizabeth Peters
1860 - 1917

Annie Laura Peters
1877 - 1951

Sarah Emeline Peters
1862 - 1929

John Henry Peters
1866 - 1957

James Conrad Peters
1840 - 1911

Christian S. Peters
1812 - 1897

Conrad Lewis Peters
1786 - 1849

Christian Peters
1760 - 1837

Anna Katharine Fudge
1766 - 1839

Clara Snidow
1790 - 1866

Mary Elizabeth Karnes
1817 - 1898

Polly Ann Thompson
1838 - 1928

Mettie Burke Peters
1868 - 1899

Edith Rebecca Peters
1880 - 1915

Fannie Snidow Peters
1870 - 1951

Lucy Jane Peters
1884 - 1889

William Karnes Peters
1873 - 1949

near Mercer Salt Works, in what is now Summers County, West Virginia but was then Mercer County, Virginia. It is difficult to determine when he made this move as there are conflicting dates of the births of some of his children, showing some born in Giles Co., Virginia, some in Monroe Co., Virginia and some in Mercer Co., Virginia. He probably moved to Mercer County a little after 1850. Christian Snidow worked near Mercer Salt Works with his friends the Shumates, in the manufacture of salt. While living near there, he served as Constable. As such, he was ordered to sell the farm and home of a friend and neighbor to enforce a judgment against him. Christian Snidow refused, saying that the judgment was unjust and unfair. To settle the matter, he substituted his own farm and sold it to satisfy the judgment.[6] After losing his farm and home, he and all his family except his two married children, Rebecca Jane and James Conrad, moved to Walton in Roane County, West Virginia. The family moved there about April of 1861, as the Civil War was starting. While living at Walton, Christian Snidow attempted to introduce the growing of tobacco to that area without much success. He and his family then moved on to Round Knob Creek in Roane County where he managed the 2200-acre plantation of Samuel Sinnett. Sinnett was a widower with four children and married Sarah Burke Peters, daughter of Christian Snidow Peters on Aug. 9, 1866. Christian Snidow moved again to Slab Fork, another nearby creek. He then lived with his youngest son, Lewis Karnes Peters until his death. Deeds and other records show that Christian Snidow never owned any of the land on which he lived in Roane County.[7] Christian Snidow Peters died near Spencer in Roane County on April 3, 1897 and is buried in the Round Knob Cemetery on Round Knob Creek in Roane County. Mary Elizabeth died the next year and is buried beside her husband. Samuel Sinnett is also buried in this same cemetery. Another of Christian Snidow's children, Nancy E. is also buried there. She married Gilbert N. Cottrell in 1868. Gilbert had fought with the 60th Virginia Infantry, CSA and has a CSA headstone. Christian Snidow Peters and Mary Elizabeth Karnes had ten children. The fourth, James Conrad Peters, was born at Peterstown on July 25, 1840.

Graves of James Peters' parents in Round Knob Cemetery,
near Spencer, Roane County, West Virginia.

Chapter II
Western Virginia Before the War

The area the Peters family called home in the first half of the 1800s was considered the frontier or the western edge of civilization. There were few brick or frame homes; most were log cabins. The people were generally common folk. That is, they were not the blue-blooded aristocrats from the Eastern Virginia tidewater area. They were the hardy pioneers in the true sense. Hard work on the farm was a way of life. Many, like Christian Peters and his brother, had received their land from Land Office Treasury Warrants either for service in the Revolution and Indian Wars, or simply bought for cheap prices at the courthouse steps in Richmond.

In this wilderness the larger rivers such as the Ohio, New, and Kanawha became the principal method of transportation. It was stated that "...west of the Alleghanies, the direction of travel and trade was largely toward the Ohio River."[1] By 1830 steamboats were plying the Ohio from Cincinnati to Pittsburgh and had opened Charleston and the Kanawha Valley to river traffic. Along the Ohio and the Kanawha were many landings, with each town having a wharf where the steamboats and keelboats put in to pick up cargo.

The western section [of Virginia] lying westward of the mountains to the Ohio River, was characterized by swift flowing rivers, the terrain being usually cut up by mountains, making plantations impossible and the use of slaves less important than in the other section. Also, in this section there were natural resources consisting of forest products, salt, and later coal. The western section was swiftly becoming an important manufacturing and commercial center demanding a good system of transportation as being essential to its development and prosperity.[2]

The better roads were called turnpikes. They were, however, only dirt roads that had been cleared wide enough for wagons to pass in some spots. The 1850s saw great expansion in these roads and turnpikes. Mail and people traveled on these overland roads such as the James River and Kanawha Turnpike, the Northwestern Turnpike, the Weston and Gauley Turnpike, and the Parkersburg and Staunton Turnpike. The nearest any of these major roads came to the Peters family in Monroe and Mercer Counties was the James River and Kanawha Turnpike which came from Guyandotte (now Huntington) on the Ohio, passed through Charleston, then down through Fayette County and through Lewisburg in Greenbrier County and on to Covington. The lesser roads, however, were described by a man who traveled them as: "...for want of room are much of the way in the beds of the streams, which are swollen by every heavy shower to raging, impassable torrents. Bridges do not exist excepting at a few points."[3]

The grandchildren of the pioneers were farmers and cattle-raisers. By the year 1850 the farmers and country living in this area were growing wheat, corn, buckwheat, some tobacco, and various fruits. They also raised horses, cattle, sheep, hogs and the necessary grains to feed these animals. Timber was a plentiful product from the lush forests in the area. Small amounts of iron ore and oil were being extracted from the ground. These products shipped to the east and midwest. The main routes were via the rivers and over the B & O Railroad and the Northwestern Virginia Railroad which

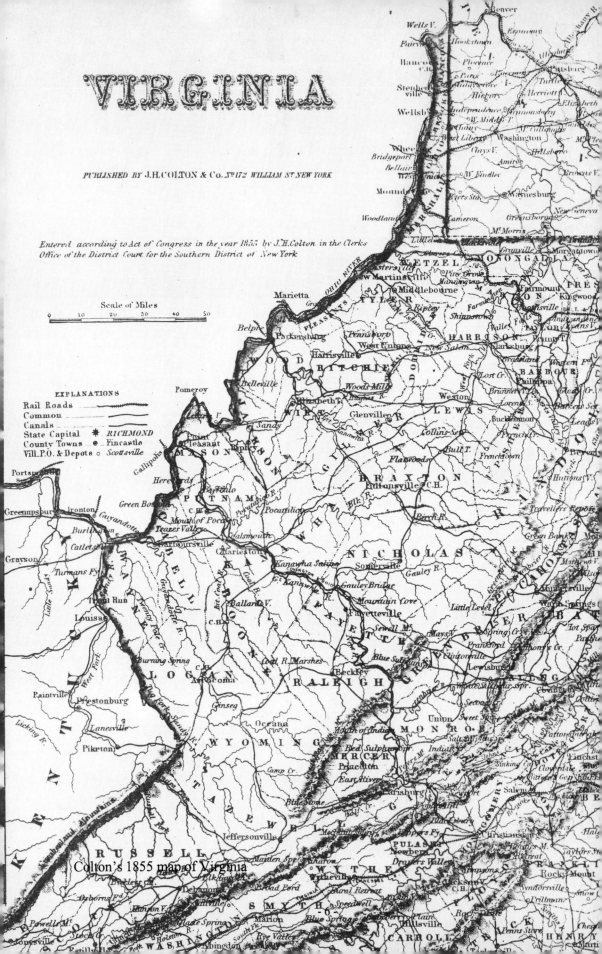

Colton's 1855 map of Virginia

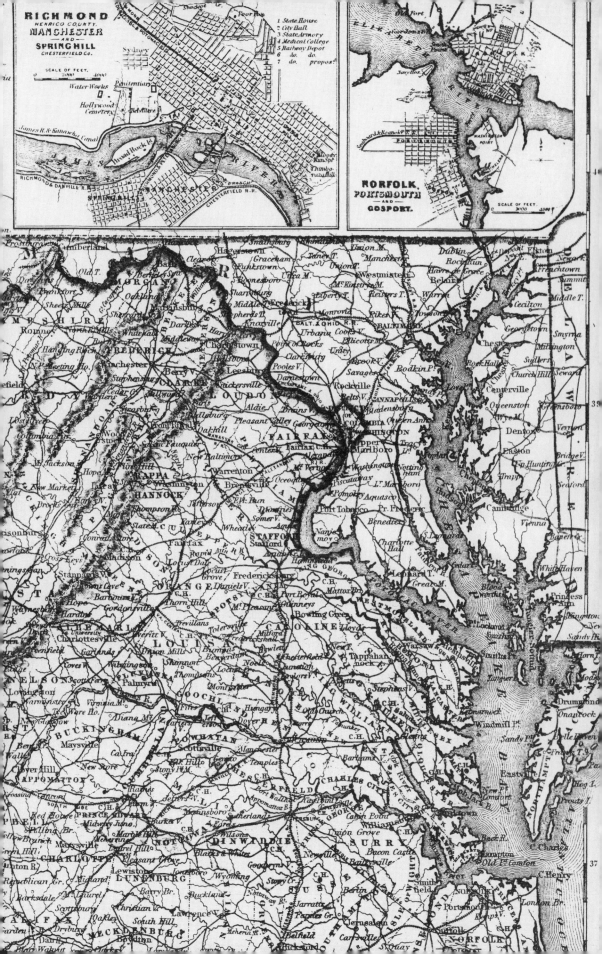

39

37

were completed in 1852 and 1857 respectively.

Every small town along a stream or river had a mill. Most were used to grind corn or grain. Molasses was produced from cane grinding mills. There were several mills in the counties of Mercer and Monroe by the late 1850s.

The towns in 1860 were small by today's standards: Wheeling was the largest with 14,083 inhabitants, Martinsburg second with a population of 3,364. Charleston had less than two thousand people, Lewisburg boasted a population of one thousand, and Harper's Ferry had a little over one thousand.[4] Parkersburg (population 2,493), Pt. Pleasant and Guyandotte were also important towns along the Ohio River.

Compared to other areas of the South, there were few slaves west of the Alleghenies. The home of the Peters family, Monroe and Mercer Counties of Virginia, had a total of only 1,476 slaves out of a total population for the two counties of 17,576 in 1860.[5] This equates to about 8.3%. The southern counties of what would become West Virginia in 1863 had a higher percentage of slaves than did the western Virginia counties overall. In 1860 only 4% of Virginia's slave population was in the western Virginia area.[6] This small percentage of slaves and slaveholders made the overall slave issue secondary to the states' rights issue in this area. As the decade of the 1850s came to a close, the good people of western Virginia were definitely split as to their loyalties to the North or South.

By the year 1860 the political climate had grown ominous and grim. Whereas in earlier decades efforts at compromise on the slavery and states' rights issues had postponed bloodshed except for a few isolated events, things had definitely changed. Now there was no middle-ground; no room for compromise. The Abolitionists took the extreme view on the one hand. In their view slavery had to be abolished totally and immediately. The pro-slavery subscribers took the opposite view: slavery was at the heart of the Southern economy and must be preserved at least until some other method of working plantations was discovered. The Northerners also believed that the Federal Government had the right to dictate which states would join the Union as free or slave. The Southerners believed that the individual states should have the right to determine this and many other directions. Neither side would give an inch. When compromise was no longer possible, it was only a matter of time before the exchange of gunfire would be heard. Neither side had long to wait.

Chapter III
James and His Family Before The War

*L*ittle *is known about* the early childhood of James Conrad Peters. He was born January 25, 1840 at Peterstown, Virginia (now West Virginia). Peterstown, a little settlement in Monroe County, Virginia had been named for James's Revolutionary War ancestor, Christian Peters. Succeeding generations of the Peters family had lived either in Peterstown or within a few miles of the village. James's father and mother, Christian Snidow Peters and Mary Elizabeth Karnes, lived at Peterstown through James' early years and at least eight of their ten children were born there. Christian Snidow Peters was a blacksmith, plantation manager, schoolteacher and music teacher.[1] Evidently he was most well-known in the area as a blacksmith. Christian Snidow also learned how to work with iron and could hammer wagon wheel rims, springs and other implements used on the farms in the area. It is certainly reasonable to believe that James Conrad learned part of this trade, being the oldest of four surviving sons in a family of ten children. (Another brother, John Karnes Peters, died in infancy.) James Conrad probably also helped in the work on the farms, as his father also managed another large farm or plantation. This second farm was that of his father-in-law, John Karnes. This farm supported cattle, horses and sheep and also produced a tobacco crop.

According to the Peters genealogy, Christian Snidow Peters moved probably in the late 1850s. "After most of his children were born, he moved to Mercer County, and settled near the Mercer Salt Works, and worked with his friends, the Shumates, in their manufacture of salt and other enterprises."[2] Since Summers County was not formed until 1871, Mercer Salt Works was in Mercer County up until that time. This move may not have been to Mercer County, however.

A look at the map showing where the three present-day counties of Mercer, Summers, and Monroe converge shows that only a few miles takes in parts of all three. In the 1850 Census of Virginia Christian S. Peters and his family are shown as living in Monroe County.[3] James C. is shown as being eleven years old. It is possible that they lived on New River but on the East (Monroe County) side at that time.

It was during these years, when James Conrad Peters was eighteen years old, that he made the first brief entry in the diary that would eventually recount episodes of this country's great struggle of 1861–65. (There was one previous entry written in a different place in the diary, but it only stated the date: "Sept. 16, 1858.")

> *September 17th*
> *1858*
> *September the 18th 1858*
> *singing school   Friday & Saturday*
> *Jas C. Peters*

Since we know that James's father taught music, it is possible that this "singing school" was conducted by his father. It is also possible that this school was taught by one of the churches in the Peterstown area. Singing and poetry did play a part in James's life, as evidenced by the poems written by James in his diary, including one song, complete with the musical notes, entitled "One Heart is Enough For Me":

(Song)

One heart is enough for me.
One heart to love adore.
One heart is enough for me.
---who could wish for more.
The birds that soar above
And sing their songs on high.
Ask but for one to love
And therefore should not I
One heart is enough for me &
James C Peters
One heart I do love adore
that heart is enough for me
I never shall wish for more
Though many miles from her
I have loved her all my life.

Pages of the diary showing the song "One Heart is Enough For Me."

We also know that James' father was active in the Methodist Church. Evidently James received and took note of the Bible and its teachings. On the same pages as the first dated entries and the song is the notation:

...Without thee my-----
20th book of Revelation
11th & 15th verses
Jas C Peters

We must assume that James meant the 20th Chapter of the Book of Revelations, as there is not a 20th book. The 15th verse of that chapter reads: "And whosoever was not found written in the Book of Life, was cast into the Lake of Fire."[4]

Then in June of 1859 detailed diary entries start that give us insight into James Conrad Peters and his occupation before the War. In the following entries, he details his travelings over central West Virginia for what appears to be the purpose of evaluating or appraising land. What education this young man of nineteen years had that prepared him for this occupation is unknown. It is logical to conclude that he must have had a good grasp of basic math and other skills. Here he was, traveling by himself over hundreds of miles of some of the roughest terrain of what is today West Virginia looking at land. He must have been a bright, competent young man to be trusted with such a task.

Left Home Monday June 13th 1859 travel 26 miles to John Lilly's
bill 7.50.

14th Travel 29 miles to John Thompson's dinner at princes bill--.66
Land holders: Ben Smith, Dr Chapman, Terry Green,
hogs, cows, ewes, horses
Isaac Staly owns 160 acres

June 15 travel to Fayette C H for dinner bill 75 c
Stay at Wm Montgomery's bill $1.00 travel 28 ms.

16th travel 26 miles to Browns town stay at Mr Jonathans house.
At James Morris's bill .50c

An examination of a West Virginia map reveals that James Conrad traveled down the New River (which actually flows North) to Fayetteville (then Fayette Courthouse or "Fayette C H"). He then followed the old James River & Kanawha Turnpike to Brownstown which is now Marmet, just outside of Charleston. He estimated his mileage along these meanderings of the New and Kanawha Rivers to be 109 miles. John Lilly was living at that time near Prince, on the Raleigh-Fayette County line, which James noted as his first night's stop. It should also be noted that James frequently wrote down what appears to have been the type of livestock that was kept at certain farms.

Friday 17.["Saturday" marked through] *Rainy.*
Traveled to John Ganolsons on Davis Creek 7 miles

Saturday 18. to Charleston 7 miles. See Ben Smith
and get directions to the head of Big Sandy.
Dinner at Dullings 37 1/2cts. Stay at Daniel Pauley's 16 ms
from Charleston.

Sunday 19. Go to W Camp−5 crossings between Charleston. The
following creeks, to wit, 2 miles Creek, Mill Creek, Indian Creek,
Pinchgut, Elk River then up Little Sandy to its head then on to
Greencreek & Rock Creek & Meadows Creek.
To Johnson's Creek to Wm Camp waters of Polka River 19 miles.

Monday 20. Leave Wm Camps travel 11 mls dined at Mr.
Ferrell Land Office. by his fathers at $3.00 improved Land Book.
Rain very hard in the evening travel 5 Miles to Mr. Quinns on Harrys
Fork branch of the west fork of the Little Kanawha & stay all night.

James was right in marking through "Saturday" for June 17, 1859 as it was indeed a Friday. From near Marmet James turns south back toward Raleigh County. The creeks he mentions, especially "Pinchgut," are in that direction. Pinch Gut is a small tributary of Glade Creek in Raleigh County. His mileage for these four days was 65 miles. Notice part of this was back-tracking to Charleston to get directions from Ben Smith. The notation about "...his fathers at $3.00 improved Land Book" is unclear. He probably used the new land book at Ferrell's Land Office to locate some of the tracts of land he was wanting to evaluate. Notice that the diary served not only as his record of who he visited, but his mileage and expense record.

Tuesday 21st. Go to Calhoun C.H. Dinner at Mr. Hays bill .50 cts.
Look at 2 tracts of land price $5.00. Meet John B. Lily and stay
all night.

Wednesday 22. Travel up the west fork of the Little Kanawha to
Thos. Jarvis to dinner. Bill 25 cts. Look at some rough land then up
White Oak to its head crossing the ridge to Sandy Waters to Wm
Cookman. Stay with Mr. Cookman till Mon marking and examining
the lands of Smith & Smith.

Monday 27. Leave Cookmans travel 15 miles to Ashley's to dinner bill
25 cts.
Go to Wm Geary's who has land for sale stay all night.

The only mileage we have recorded here is the 15 miles on Monday, June 27. The "Calhoun C. H." he mentions is now Grantsville, the county seat of Calhoun County. James notes on a neighboring page that "Post office of Wm Cookman is Newton,

Roane [County], Virginia." Some two years later James's father and mother would move to Newton, probably due to James' familiarity with the area. Newton is just inside the Roane-Clay County line. Roane, Clay, and Calhoun are neighboring counties northeast of Charleston.

28th June—travel back 3 miles look at 3 farms 1st 240 acres
bill 5.00 per acre 2nd 200 acres price 6.00 per acre. One of 900 price
4.50. Come back take dinner & leave. Travel 12 ms stay at Mr.
Youngs bill 50.

June 29. Leave Youngs travel 4 miles----Breakfast at Jarrets bill .50.
Travel 10 miles to dinner at Dullings bill .50. 2 miles to Charleston.
See B. Smith and get his prices for land on Big Sandy then 7
miles to John Garretsons stay all night.

June 30. Then go to Wm Shrewsburys stay to dinner. Go to R.
Garretsons stay all night.

July 1. Leave R Garretsons travel 13 miles to Thos. Perdue's for
lunch.(?) 13 miles then 7 miles to Pat Purdues. Stay all night.

July 2 travel 16 miles to Pat Huldrens for dinner. Stay at Bots(?)

James traveled a total of 87 miles over these four days. He was back in Charleston to get prices for more land. Following these journal entries are a list of tracts of land and the acreage contained in the tracts:

	no.	acres
T Rose tract sec	2	287
Grahams tract	4	
tract no 21		385
Taming(?) A Rodgers		
Thomas Truman tract		
No 16.		
A Newman tract	15	307
Walter George "	17	426
Gras luke(?) "	8	294

This is obviously a tally of various tracts and acres, but we know nothing more about who the people were or where the tracts were located.

July 4
back to.... traveled 22 miles to Maj. John Hagans
dinner at J Mitchells stay with Hagan all night.

5th. travel 10 miles to Sally Thompsons & spend

this day & next travel (?) evening....the morning.....

7th. travel 32 miles back to B. Holdrens.
8th. travel 35 miles to D Cooks.
9th. 25 miles to Esq Philips.
10th. 30 miles to D. Parks.

The records here for the 4th through the 10th of July, 1859 are sparse. James traveled 154 miles in this seven day period. On the 7th through the 10th he averaged traveling 30.5 miles per day. Over the terrible roads or paths and on horseback, he indeed did some grueling traveling. Probably he was so tired by evening that he had little zest for recording all the facts of his days' work. The next few pages of the diary show a tally of something for several people. There is nothing to tell us what the tally is for. Following these few pages of the tally are some accounting entries. The first reads: "A. J. Thompson dr." This ends his entries for his work in the summer of 1859. It is odd that he seemed to stop in the middle of a trip, as he makes no mention of returning home.

It is possible that during this trip James met a young lady, Polly Ann Thompson. She was the daughter of Andrew Jackson Thompson (shown as "A. J." in many records) and Elizabeth French and was born Nov. 16, 1838 in Mercer County. James Conrad Peters and Polly Ann Thompson were married Sept. 29, 1859 in Mercer County by Abraham Garretson. It is possible that this was one of the Garretsons mentioned in James' travels of that summer.

Exactly where James and Polly Ann lived the first few years of their married life is unclear. They were enumerated in the household with James's parents in the 1860 census of Monroe County, taken on June 14, 1860. The occupation of both James and his father was given as farmer.[5] Also in the household was James's grandmother, Clara Peters, who was 70 years old. Perhaps James and Polly were visiting his grandmother at the time. The only location given on the census was Peterstown District.

Certainly by this time the events that were dividing the country and southwestern Virginia in two factions on the brink of war were having profound effects on James and his young family. Discussions and debates were taking place wherever people met. Sometimes fist-fights erupted over the heated arguments that resulted.

A blessed event occurred in James and Polly's lives on Sept. 13, 1860. Their first child, a daughter named Mary Elizabeth, was born. Mary Elizabeth never married and cared for her parents in their later years.

In the months following the birth of Mary Elizabeth, James's father took his family, except for James Conrad and his oldest daughter, Rebecca Jane, and left the area. Rebecca Jane had married William Henderson Thompson on Oct. 6, 1858. James Conrad and Rebecca Jane were the only two married children as of 1860 and this explains why they remained behind. Christian and the remainder of his family arrived at Walton in Roane County in April, 1861, the same month the Civil War erupted.[6] He and his wife would live out the remainder of their lives in Roane County.

Little could the Peters family suspect what the events of the next few years would bring to their lives and to the lives of their friends and neighbors.

Chapter IV
James Signs Up - First Year of the War

By the spring of 1861, war loomed on the horizon. At discussion meetings, often held in churches or schools, fist fights or small riots would break out over the arguments of the day. As both sides began recruiting military companies in the same towns hostilities erupted between neighbors and even within families.

> Enlistments were rapidly going on in all the counties, cities, towns, and villages within the Commonwealth, and the people of the New River Valley counties were abreast with their sister counties in this great movement.[1]

It needs to be understood at this point that as the first shots were fired and volunteers began flocking to the recruiters for both sides, those men who enlisted from Virginia were not enrolling in Confederate service. Rather they were enrolling as volunteers in their state forces or "State Service." Therefore the men of Virginia who enlisted were enlisting in the Virginia State Forces, which were being mobilized by Governor John Letcher. Most of the men from the western Virginia counties simply saw their duty as the defense of their homes and their state from a Northern invasion. They also were promised in many cases by the recruiters that they would be allowed to stay in the immediate area of their homes. Indeed, no one at this early date could foresee the widespread geographical scope the War would encompass over the next four years.

The officers who recruited the Virginia volunteer forces in most of the counties were the well-known and usually better educated men of the area. Such a man was Napoleon Bonaparte French. Born in 1811 in Giles County, Virginia, French had been deputy sheriff until his marriage to Jane Armstrong. Napoleon and his family then moved to Mercer County and established a store, mill and eventually a post office which was named Frenchville (now Oakvale) after him. He then served in both the Senate and House of Delegates in the Virginia Legislature. He was also elected by Mercer County to the Virginia Secession Convention, where he voted for secession. French was an important political figure, and one of the richest men in Mercer County by 1861.[2] His real estate was valued at $15,000 in the 1860 census.

Other officers in the volunteer forces had previously served in the Virginia Militia. Officers in the militia were commissioned by the governor upon the recommendation of the county courts. These officers were the socially prominent men of their county, and being an officer in the militia was considered a honorable position. Such a man was John S. Carr. In 1861 Carr was the Lt. Col. of the 151st Virginia Militia which was the regiment from Mercer County.

So it was that on July 27, 1861, Napoleon French and John Carr met with a group of seventy-five men who wished to enlist as a company of cavalry in the Virginia Volunteers. One of these seventy-five men was James Conrad Peters. Carr, due to his rank in the Militia, was the recognized officer at this meeting and he signed the enlistment papers of the men as their enrolling officer.[3]

The site the men chose to rally for their enlistment was the Alvis Farm, located

Grave of Napoleon B. French in Rest Haven Cemetery, Princeton, Mercer County, W.V. He was captain and organizer of French's Battery and later captain of Company B, 30th Battalion Virginia Sharpshooters.

between Elgood and Princeton in the eastern end of Mercer County.

The unit these brave men formed that day in July became known as Napoleon B. French's Company, Virginia Volunteers. The unit bore French's name as he was recognized as its organizer, and French was elected its captain. In the Virginia Volunteer companies, the officers were elected by the men and then approved in Richmond. This was a cavalry unit, and many of the men furnished their own horses. We believe that James Conrad Peters furnished his own horse, due to the supplies he received.

The men returned to their homes for a few weeks. During that time, a dispatch was sent from Gen. Alfred Beckley to Gen. Robert E. Lee. It was dated Aug. 21, 1861, and contained interesting information relating to French's Company:

> ...understanding there were four companies of volunteers newly
> organized...in the county of Mercer in the vicinity of Princeton, viz two
> companies of cavalry, under Capts. Napoleon B. French & William H. French.
> These captains refused to be mustered [into the 35th Infantry Regiment]....[4]

Alfred Beckley had served as Colonel of the 27th Brigade of Virginia Militia before the War. He was appointed a Colonel of Virginia Volunteers in August, and was attempting to organize a regiment to be designated the 35th Infantry Volunteer Regiment. This regiment, however, was never organized. His statement does show that both Napoleon and his brother, William H., were determined to keep their units as cavalry and wanted them to either remain independent, or to be attached to a cavalry regiment, and not Beckley's infantry regiment.

The men assembled and were formally mustered in at Princeton in Mercer County on Sept. 20, 1861. James Conrad Peters appears on the muster rolls that day as a private.[5] French's newly formed unit was assigned to Brig. Gen. John B. Floyd's command. On August 11, 1861, Gen. Floyd had taken command of the Army of the Kanawha.[6] Floyd was an ex-governor of Virginia, as was another Confederate officer in the western Virginia area, Brig. Gen. Henry A. Wise. These two generals would argue and disagree over command questions through August and September. On September 10, Floyd's army had been defeated at the Battle of Carnifex Ferry in Nicholas County.

Brig. Gen. John B. Floyd, CSA
Commander of Floyd's Brigade before Fort Donelson,
Senior commander at Fort Donelson, TN, February 1862
Courtesy West Virginia State Archives

The men then went into camp and began to collect their equipment and to drill. It was probably during this time that James received the items that he listed in his diary. With no other explanation he listed these in his diary:

Received of the Southern Confederacy

1 cap	*1 pair pants*
2 shirts	*1 coat*
1 overcoat	*2 pair drawers*
1 blanket	*1 oil cloth*
1 saddle blanket	
1 haversack	*1 nose bag*
1 pair boots	*1 pair spurs*
1 cartridge box & cap box & belt	
1 curry comb & brush	
1 canteen	*1 circingle*
1 bridle & martingale	
1 tin cup	*1 plate*
1 shot gun	

Much of this equipment was necessary for the handling of a cavalry horse. The martingale was part of the strapping that passed under the horse's neck, between his forelegs and was attached to its belly strap. The circingle (or surcingle) was the belt or band that passed around the body of the horse and helped secure the saddle. We might assume that since a saddle was not on the list of items he received, that James Conrad provided his own saddle with his horse. It is also interesting that the weapon which was issued to him was a shotgun. It was a popular theory at the beginning of the War that the cavalry would be doing close-in fighting or conducting charges against infantry or gun emplacements, and therefore the shotgun would be a logical choice in place of a rifle or musket. Since there were very few actual large cavalry charges in the Civil War, this theory was later disproven. Most of the Confederate cavalry from western Virginia fought merely as dismounted infantry or served as couriers and scouts.

> *Sept. 25 1861*
> *Left home & went to Giles C H stayed 5 weeks & came to Mercer*
> *camped 2 weeks at Frenchville stayed at home 5 weeks. Changed*
> *our company from cavalry to artillery been in service 3 months.*

By following this brief account of the twelve weeks between July 27 and Sept. 25, we learn that James and his cavalry unit camped near Giles Courthouse (Pearisburg, the county seat of Giles County, Virginia), then spent two weeks at Frenchville (now Oakvale, Mercer County), the home of their captain, Napoleon French. They were then allowed to stay at home for a month, probably immediately preceding their muster on Sept. 20 at Princeton. Also interesting here is the simple sentence that states James' company was "changed from cavalry to artillery." The change must have taken place in the field in September, but it took two more months before the paperwork was processed in Richmond. Special Order No. 240, which officially changed the unit's designation, was issued on November 26.[7] As the War drug on, this time lag would become more pronounced between organizational changes made in the field and the formal orders being issued.

These "light" artillery units were simply field artillery that traveled with the infantry troops in the field. The cannon of these units were drawn by horses. The men of these units generally walked. It appears from later diary entries that perhaps James and his compatriots were allowed to keep their horses. If the men did indeed keep their cavalry horses, they would have been more properly denoted as "flying" or "horse" artillery. Virginia sent more light artillery units to the field than any other state, Union or Confederate.[8]

The unit was now formally known as Capt. Napoleon B. French's Battery Virginia Light Artillery. It was also known as the Mercer Artillery.

Va Ga La Miss SC Fla Ala
Tenn NC Tex Ark

A few pages prior to the Sept. 25th diary entry is this list of state abbreviations. It is a list of all the Confederate States that had seceded by the end of June, 1861. Kentucky and Missouri, which James did not include in his list, have been classified as "Border States." Missouri's legislature did pass an ordinance of secession on October 31, 1861, although it was never submitted to a vote of the people, and the people of Kentucky in a partial assembly did pass the ordinance on November 8, 1861.[9]

Since enlistment James and his comrades of French's unit had drilled, marched and camped. While they acclimated themselves to army life and thought of what would come, events were occurring in western Kentucky that would soon draw French's men to their meeting with destiny.

General Albert S. Johnston, Confederate commander in Kentucky and Tennessee, was establishing defenses to prevent the Union Army from moving on Nashville. Part of this strategy was to establish forts on the rivers, as the Union force was then massed at Cairo, Illinois. By the end of November, two batteries of artillery had been located near a little town called Dover on the Tennessee side of the Cumberland River.[10] During December and January, the batteries were prepared and earthworks were built with rifle-pits to guard the approaches. This fort that was taking shape was named Fort Donelson. Another fort was also erected some twenty miles to the west on the Tennessee River, and known as Fort Henry. "It was a thin line of gray which held the western frontier for the Confederacy."[11]

While French's men were at home or drilling, Gen. Floyd had retreated from the Kanawha Valley to Dublin Depot in Pulaski County, Virginia. He arrived there about December 9. The depot was an important supply point due to its location on the Virginia and Tennessee Railroad. Through most of the war, Dublin acted as an assembly point for Confederate forces, and a collection point for their supplies.

During this period, the men were allowed to return to their homes in Mercer County until the middle of December. On December 13, the men left their homes and marched to Dublin Depot to meet up with Gen. Floyd and his infantry.

December 22nd 1861
Left home 13th traveled 3 days to Dublin Depot & encamped.
Received our cannon 2 smooth bore and 1 rifled. Cannon had
six horses----. Have had good weather but it looks like snow
today in the---so it is not------such by many I have been bereft---
I have had a------day for-----days. This makes me feel
very weak but thank God I am still alive.

When Capt. French and the men of his unit arrived on December 16th, they received their cannon, which James Conrad noted to be two smoothbore and one rifled. For a large part of the War, the principal cannon in the field would be the smoothbore field-piece that was capable of delivering a 6-pound shot. These two smoothbore pieces were therefore probably those commonly referred to as the "6-pound Napoleon." There was also a slightly larger version that delivered a 9-pound shot. Each cannon had a caisson which was used to carry ammunition and the cleaning and ramming tools necessary to charge, load, and clean the cannon. According to James each was pulled by six horses. Sometime during the month of December, the men would pick up a fourth cannon.[12] Also on December 16th, Gen. Floyd received orders to join Gen. Albert S. Johnston at Bowling Green, Kentucky.

James noted that he had been sick for some period of time as he stated something had made him feel very weak. Camp life and lack of sanitation attributed to much of the sickness among the soldiers on both sides. Many men suffered and died from common diseases such as measles and dysentery.

The men are cooking dinner. I feel lonesome although I am
surrounded by friends. My wife & child is far away & my
heart is with them.

As Christmas Eve drew near, it was natural for the men to think of home and their families. James stated the truth learned by many over the centuries; that one can be surrounded even by friends and still feel lonesome. The child that he mentions was Mary Elizabeth, who would have been sixteen months old that Christmas.

Dec. 28th.
Nothing of importance have occurred this week. Yesterday about 12
o'clock we got orders to go to Kentucky & we loaded our cannon on
the cars. Next morning at 8 o'clock we took the cars & rolled away
& traveled to Bristol a distance of 100 miles arrived there at 8 o'clock
at night & slept in the cars.

Next morning Dec 30th we rolled away to the bridge at Holston River
10 miles & we unloaded cars & crossed over to Union. Stayed all
night & loaded our things on the cars.

The orders that the men of Floyd's Brigade including French's Battery would leave Virginia was not a surprise. There had been rumors circulating around Christmas that the Virginia units would be sent West.[13] So after noon on Friday the 27th of December, 1861, James Conrad Peters and his compatriots hauled their four field pieces and associated equipment up into the railroad cars. Evidently the men stayed in camp at Dublin until about 8 a.m. the next morning when they also boarded the train and "rolled away."

The Virginia and Tennessee Railroad carried the men in a southwesterly direction from Dublin through Wytheville, the county seat of Wythe County; on through Marion, the county seat of Smyth County; through Abingdon the county seat of Washington County and then to Bristol on the Virginia-Tennessee state line. James stated this was about 100 miles. So far the trip by rail had been a very direct route. To get to their final destination, however, the route would now become more circuitous.

At about this same time, other Virginia soldiers boarded the train bound for Bowling Green. Col. John McCausland and his two infantry regiments, the 36th and 50th Virginia Infantry Regiments, boarded either the same train at Abingdon, Virginia, or one two days later.[14] Many of the men in both of these units were from the western Virginia counties, and might have known James Peters or Napoleon French.

Probably at Bristol, the train with our men, cannon and horses crossed over onto the tracks of the East Tennessee and Georgia Railroad. The rails now turned south toward present-day Johnson City, Tennessee. Near this point was the small Tennessee town of Union.

By the fact that James recorded that they "unloaded the cars" when they stopped at Union, we can deduce from other diary entries that this probably meant unloading the tents and horses. Likewise the next morning the soldiers reloaded their equipment on the railroad cars to continue their journey.

> *Dec 31st. We got up this morning & got breakfast & struck tents*
> *& are now waiting for the trains to get ready. The freight train*
> *has just come in & has but 4 box cars that has run off tracks*
> *and cannot start with----moved.*

So on New Year's Eve the army moved just like any other day. The men cooked breakfast and took down the tents and waited for transportation. Evidently the train did not arrive without incident as it appears to have partially derailed. Tracks across different railroads during the Civil War many times presented problems. Although all the tracks so far on their trip were the common (at least in the South) five-foot gauge, alignment problems were still not uncommon.

The men of French's Battery would therefore spend New Year's Eve waiting near this small town in Tennessee for what the year of 1862 would bring. No doubt the men once again thought of their loved ones at home, which must now seem worlds away.

Roster of Mercer County Men
Enlisting July 27, 1861
in Napoleon B. French's Company Virginia Volunteers
(later French's Battery Virginia Light Artillery, CSA)

Archer, John W.	FD*	Died: 1917
Armentrout, George F.		Died: 1/14/63
Armontrout, Lee A.	FD	Died postwar
Blankenship, Winston	FD	MIA: 5/15/64
Brown, John Wesley	FD	Died: 1903
Brown, Lewis		Died: 1919
Brown, Theodore P.	FD	MWIA & Died: 6/25/64
Caldwell, John W.		Died: 1/1862
Cannaday, Fleming S. (Giles Co., Virginia)		Died: 2/17/62
Carr, William R.	FD	Died: 1910
Cole, Augustus W., Jr.		
Comer, Augustus W.		
Comer, Jacob	FD	Died: 9/1880
Comer, James	FD	Died: Ft Delaware, 4/65
Comer, John	FD	Died: Camp Douglas, 3/62
Day, James L.	FD	Died: 9/30/62
Fisher, Balis	FD	
Fisher, James Henry	FD	
Fisher, John	FD	Died: Camp Douglas, 3/62
Fisher, Joseph	FD	
French, Jehu E.	FD	Died: 1888
French, Napoleon B.		Died: 1899
Garretson, William		
Haslip, James L.		Died postwar
Johnson, Daniel B.	FD	Died postwar
Johnson, Doctor P.	FD	Died postwar
Johnson, Joseph W.		
Johnson, Samuel	FD	Died postwar
Lilly, Robert C.	FD	Died: 1905
Maitland, John J.	FD	
Meadows, Floyd W.		Died: 4/29/62
Melvin, Rufus W.		
Miller, Frank J.	FD	
Neale, Daniel Newton		Died: 1917
Oney, William H.		KIA Ft. Donelson 2/14/62
Pendleton, Benjamin	FD	Died: 9/13/62
Pendleton, David B.	FD	Died: 1902
Pendleton, Wyatt W.	FD	Died: 1898
Pennington, Elliott		Died: 1914
Peters, James Conrad	FD	Died: 1/9/1911

Reed, Thomas		Died: 1905
Russell, James H.		
Russell, William		
Sarver, Henry	FD	Died postwar
Sarver, John		Died postwar
Shannon, John R.	FD	
Shumaker, John J.	FD	Died postwar
Smith, Charles R.		
Smith, Daniel L.		
Smith, Isaac A.	FD	Died postwar
Smith, John W.	FD	Died postwar
Smith, Joseph T.	FD	
Smith, Theodore, Jr.	FD	Died postwar
Sower, John	FD	
Steele, William French	FD	Died: 1929
Tanner, Frederick		Died: 11/10/62
Thomas, Boston W.		Died postwar
Thomas, George P.		Died: 8/7/1866
Thomas, Green	FD	
Thomas, Henderson F.		
Thomas, James H.	FD	
Thomas, Lampkin McKinney		
Thornton, Andrew J.		Died: 4/1906
Thornton, James A.		
Thornton, Thomas P.	FD	Died: Camp Douglas 9/62
Tiller, Hiram		
Tiller, Thomas J.		
Tiller, William A.	FD	
Tracy, Edward George	FD	
Tracy, Harvey S.	FD	
Tracy, Roland	FD	Died: Vicksburg 9/21/62
Turner, Robert B.	FD	Died: 12/1892
White, James Russel		Died: 3/1908
Woolwine, Joseph W.		Died: 1888
Wright, Camden G.		Died: 1900

* Those men who were captured at Ft. Donelson, Tennessee Feb. 16, 1862.

Chapter V
Camp Life and Fort Donelson

January 1st 1862
We left Union at sunset & traveled 30 miles to Lime stone got
there at 9 o'clock stayed all night & started next morning at
daylight & traveled about 100 miles to Knoxville; stayed all night,
slept in cars.

New Years Day 1862 found Peters and his comrades again on the bouncing, jostling train cars. It is safe to say that none of the men of French's Battery realized that they were making history. One of the "firsts" of the Civil War was the serious and strategic use of the railroads to transport troops and supplies during wartime. The young artillerists had more practical concerns and thoughts while rolling through the hills and valleys of Tennessee on the train. Certainly they were skeptical about leaving their native Virginia soil. They also no doubt wondered what faced them at their destination. The officers were no doubt concerned that the green troops had not yet loaded or fired their cannon.

The short trip to Limestone, Tennessee ended at 9 p.m. when the train ground to a halt. Limestone was located about 21 miles southwest of Johnson City. Since James Peters stated the battery started at daylight the next day [January 2nd] they probably did not unload the horses or any equipment from the train that night.

The next day the train made better time, covering about 100 miles from Limestone to Knoxville, Tennessee. Once again, the men could not unload supplies or horses and they spent the night sleeping in the railroad cars. At least the train was sitting still, and the men were not attempting to sleep while being jostled over the rails.

Somewhere along this route the men of French's Battery were joined by Capt. John Henry Guy's Goochland Artillery. This unit was from Goochland County, Virginia and was also known as the Goochland Light Artillery or Capt. Guy's Company Virginia Artillery.[1] The Goochland Artillery was also equipped with four cannon.

Capt. French was absent from the battery, having been left somewhere along the way due to illness.[2] Commanding the unit, therefore, was Lt. John J. Maitland, who had enlisted with James Peters and his comrades on that fateful day at the Alvis Farm. Since Maitland had also resided in Mercer County before the War, he was probably at least an acquaintance if not a friend of James Peters.

Got up next morning & took our horses off cars & fed them & about
2 o'clock we put our horses on the cars & at 10 o'clock at night we
left Knoxville & traveled to Chattanooga about 120 miles.

On the 3rd of January Peters and his comrades were able to off-load the horses and feed them. It is doubtful that the men were able to see any of the city of Knoxville because by early afternoon the order came to load the horses back on the cars. Finally at 10 p.m. the train rolled out of Knoxville and chugged the 120 miles to Chattanooga. Probably this "midnight run" took most of the night over the uneven tracks. At least at

Chattanooga the men received a small reward in the form of some good home-cooked food:

> *Had breakfast prepared for us & very kind people. Left there at 8*
> *o'clock at night & traveled to Nashville 150 miles & started on to*
> *Bowling Green. Went about 30 miles & came back to N[ashville]*
> *& stayed all night & I have been taking a look at the town & am*
> *now sitting on the Capitol steps with the city all before me with*
> *those lines we expect to leave at 1 o'clock for Bowling G[reen]*

When the train left Chattanooga, it proceeded a short distance in a southwesterly direction into northern Alabama to the little junction town of Stevenson, Alabama. At Stevenson the tracks split, and the train turned north onto the tracks of the Nashville and Chattanooga Railroad. This route that Peters gives as being 150 miles now brought the train north through Murfreesboro and into the Tennessee capital of Nashville. When they rolled about thirty miles out of the city of Nashville, something happened that caused them to backtrack to the capital. About thirty miles by rail from Nashville was the crossroads of Gallatin, Tennessee and perhaps something happened to the schedule or maybe there were problems with switching. At least the men now had time to walk through the largest town they had passed through since leaving their farms in far-away Mercer County. It obviously impressed James Conrad to be sitting on the

BOWLING-GREEN KY.

College Hill, and Fortification in the distance.   Pike Bridge, destroyed by the Rebels.

View of Bowling Green, KY, as it looked to James and his compatriots in January of 1862. *Harper's Weekly*

capitol steps and looking out "...with the city all before me." The capitol building itself was certainly impressive, having been completed in 1855. By that time Nashville also was the major railroad center for the state. In 1860 the population of Nashville was over 32,000. The city would certainly have been a memorable sight to the farm boys. Since Peters made no mention of details of either Knoxville or Chattanooga we must assume, therefore, that the men did not have a chanch to tour those towns.

January 6th 1862
Left N[ashville] at 1 o'clock last night & arrived at Bowling Green
about 12 o'clock & went into camp 2 1/2 miles from B[owling]
G[reen] NW.

When the train left Nashville, heading now due north back into Kentucky, they were moving on the tracks of the Louisville & Nashville Railroad. At last the train rolled into the station at Bowling Green, Kentucky. This was the major assembly point for the Confederate Army in western Kentucky. Confederate Generals Hardee and Buckner both had entire divisions encamped there. Gen. Floyd's Virginia troops began to arrive at Bowling Green with this detraining of French's and Guy's Batteries. The two batteries arrived on January 6th, and Col. John McCausland and his infantry arrived two days later. By January 9th, all of Floyd's Brigade was at Bowling Green. These would be the last Confederate troops to arrive at the camp. Their arrivals brought

Railroad Bridge, destroyed by the Rebels.

total Confederate troop strength at Bowling Green to about 21,000 men.[3]

While the distance between Dublin, Virginia and Bowling Green, Kentucky is only about 330 miles as the crow flies, neither railroads, surface roads or any other method of travel during Civil War times went in anything that resembled a straight line. James Conrad Peters' mileage recorded in his diary adds up to be 510 miles from Dublin to Nashville. (He neglected to estimate the mileage by rail from Nashville to Bowling Green; a distance of approximately sixty miles.) Their meanderings by rail had taken the men through Virginia, Tennessee, a corner of Alabama, north through Tennessee again and finally into Kentucky. Rail travel for troops during the War may have been important, but it certainly wasn't direct as the travel of James and his comrades proves.

As French's Battery began to work on their encampment 2.5 miles northwest of Bowling Green, work was continuing at a rapid pace on Ft. Donelson to the west. By January, the fort was surrounded by an abatis of felled timber and some rifle pits had been dug. At least two cannon batteries were mounted. The troops and engineers working there had also built 400 log huts for winter quarters.[4]

> *Jan 7th. Occupied today in fixing up camp & writing home & c.*
> *Jan 8th. Went to depot after guns & got wet. Rained all evening.*
> *Jan 9th. Spent the day fixing up camp.*
> *" 10th. Drill a little today & knock around.*
> *" 11th. Drill & wash clothes today & fix up for Sunday our captain came in today.*

Here for the first time since beginning their long train trip on December 28th, James had an opportunity to pen a letter home. Probably the "fixing up camp" on January 7th consisted of unloading tents and supplies and putting up their tents. Evidently their cannon remained on the railcars at Bowling Green until James and his crew went after them. The next few days consisted of drilling and more fixing up of the camp. On Saturday, January 11, Capt. Napoleon French came into camp, having recovered from his illness.

The drilling James referred to consisted of marching and perhaps small arms training. The men had not yet been able to train in the handling and firing of their cannon.

> *Sunday January 12th 1862*
> *I went to preaching today held at the 51st Regiment by its chaplain.*
> *Preached from John 1st chapter & 1st verse. Administered Lord's*
> *Supper very civil congregation. Warm day but windy.*
>
> *" 13th. Commenced to cleanup new camp ground.*
> *" 14th. Worked at camp ground. Bad weather.*
> *" 15th. Moved to new camp 3 qtr miles from old (north). Very bad day rainy.*
> *" 16th. Built chimney to tent & drill in the evening looks like snow.*

In keeping with James' religious training before the war, he found the opportunity to attend a service conducted on his first Sunday in camp. It was conducted by Chaplain

J. P. Garland of the 51st Virginia Infantry.[5] The 51st Virginia was another of Gen. Floyd's Virginia units, commanded by Col. Gabriel C. Wharton. For the second time, Peters noted an exact Bible verse in his diary. The scripture used by Garland at this service was John 1:1: "In the beginning was the Word, and the Word was with God, and the Word was God."[6] We also must assume from James' comment about administering of the "Lord's Supper-very civil congregation" that James did take communion on that Sunday morning, and that the men in attendance were at least in a serious or "civil" mood. That Sunday was warm for a day in January.

The next two days were spent working around the camp, while the weather turned bad. Why the men had to pack up and move the entire camp 3/4 of a mile north on a bad rainy day was not mentioned. On the 16th of January, James and his tentmates spent their time building a chimney for their tent. This construction may sound rather frightening when we think of a tent with a fire burning in a chimney, but this was a accepted technique to keep the occupants warm, if more permanent structures could not be built. Having a fire that night must have been welcome as James noted it "...looks like snow."

> *January 1862*
> *17th. Drill to day.*
> *18th. Rained all this day. Occupied myself writing home.*
>
> *Sunday 19th. Spent this day in camp. Received an order in the evening to prepare for review by Gen. Hardee & went to work.*
>
> *20th. Went on parade for review but day too bad. Gen. did not come.*
> *21st. Went on parade again today but the General did not come today again.*
>
> *22nd. Stay in camp to day. Received orders in evening to prepare to move in the morning at 8 o'clock.*

Once again James took time on a rainy day in camp to write home. Since he had made no mention up to this point of receiving mail from home, we must assume that due to his traveling over the last month the poor Confederate mail system had not caught up with him and he had not heard from home.

James and his comrades continued to drill and the next Sunday they received orders to prepare for a review by Gen. Hardee. Major Gen. William J. Hardee at that time was the commander of all the units at Bowling Green. His army, designated as the Central Army of Kentucky, now included Gen. Floyd and his Virginia troops. Hardee was an experienced officer, having served in the Mexican War and graduated from West Point. He was the author of *Rifle and Light Infantry Tactics* (better known simply as *"Hardee's Tactics"*) which was one of the standard textbooks of the troops on both sides. Hardee was one of the original lieutenant generals authorized by the Confederacy.[7] Hardee's superior was Gen. Albert Sidney Johnston who commanded Department Number 2 of the Confederacy, which basically stretched from the Alleghenies westward to Oklahoma.

Typical of army life are the next three days, which saw James and the battery cleaning up their camp and then on two consecutive days they assembled in parade formation only to hear that Gen. Hardee was not coming. Perhaps Generals Hardee and Johnston had to attend to problems in other areas of their vast jurisdiction. On the third day the men wisely stayed in camp.

> *January 23rd 1862   Bowling Green, Kentucky*
> *Cool morning received orders last night not to move until tomorrow.*
>
> *24th. Shipped our guns on the cars & part of us took our horses &*
> *started to Russellville. Traveled to Sink Hole Mill & camped.*
>
> *25th. Started at daylight this morning traveled 30 miles to*
> *Russellville & met with the rest of our men & guns & camped.*
> *Felt unwell today.*
>
> *26th Sunday. Stayed about camp today put ammunition in caissons*
> *& felt unwell today but hope to be better by the blessing of God.*

So after receiving orders to move the morning of January 23rd, additional orders were issued not to move until the 24th. The battery loaded their cannon and caissons on the railcars, while James and at least some of his comrades mounted their horses and headed overland for Russellville. They camped the night of the 24th at Sinkhole Mill. Meanwhile the train rolled south out of Bowling Green. A few miles south the rails forked at a crossroads known as Memphis Junction. There the train turned southwest to Russellville. At daylight on the 25th, James and his men mounted their horses and rode the remaining thirty miles into Russellville, where they met up with the rest of the battery and evidently off-loaded their cannon and supplies.

The little town of Russellville in Logan County, Kentucky, was known as the "Confederate capital of Kentucky." While Kentucky had struggled to remain neutral through 1861, the state had still voted to join the Union. There was strong Confederate sentiment in Kentucky, however, and in November of 1861 the southern delegates had assembled at Russellville and formed what they called the Provisional Government of Kentucky.[8] In December, this provisional government went through the motions of having Kentucky admitted into the Confederate States. Even though the delegates selected Bowling Green to be the seat of this second state government, many meetings continued to be held in Russellville. The town was described as: "...a beautiful little southern town."[9]

On Saturday and again on Sunday, James felt "unwell." This did not prevent him from packing the cannon's powder and shot and rammers into the caissons on Sunday. This was a necessary step before taking their guns into action or for field exercises. Each cannon had its caisson that was on a small trailer pulled behind the gun. It carried a large wooden case or trunk for storing the powder and various ball or canister that would be needed by the artillerymen.

Russelville, Kentucky
January 27th 1862.
Drill to day. Felt better. Time half out today. Cloudy weather.

28th. Fired our cannon at target today &c.
29th. Rained all today stay in camp bad times.
30th. Cold & snowing. Received letter from home. Wrote back in
the evening.

31st. Washed clothes today stayed about camp & sent a letter to the
office which I wrote yesterday. Two men came from hospital to camp.

James' health had improved by Monday, January 27. The day was cloudy, and the men drilled for a short time and then had half the day off for relaxation.

The next day was significant in that for the first time since receiving their cannon, the men actually conducted target practice with the big guns. This was no doubt an exciting experience as the guns boomed out their earth-shaking reports. Certainly the residents of the little town of Russellville could hear this artillery fire booming over their houses. This practice was necessary not only for the men to have experience in how to accurately aim and fire, but also to gain experience in the several steps that had to be executed in an exact sequence to clean, load, and fire the cannon.

On January 29th, typical late January weather begin to set in around the camp. First rain and the next day snow fell over camp. Peters called it "bad times." The 30th was a good day, however, in spite of the cold and snow, as James received probably his first letter from home since leaving Virginia. It is possible that James received the great news in this letter that he would be a father for the second time! Unless he had been told by his wife, Polly Ann, before leaving in early December, this would have been his first communication from her. Depending on when the letter was actually written, Polly Ann would have been about three or four months pregnant. James quickly wrote back that evening, but did not get his letter posted at the office before it closed, so he posted it the next day, being a Friday and the last day of January, 1862.

The last day of January was also occupied with some of the more mundane duties of camp life, such as washing clothes. His comment about two men returning from a hospital to camp was also indicative of the hazards of camp life at that time. Other Confederate units at Bowling Green and Russellville reported hundreds of men on the "sick lists." Some of the diseases that plagued the men are virtually unheard of today, such as mumps, measles, and dysentery.

Russelville, Logan Co., Kentucky
February 1st. 1862
Went 3 qtr. miles to prepare a new camp & built chimney & c.
2nd, Sunday. Moved to new camp today bad day, cold snowing
& rainy.

3d. Bad day stay in camp. Fix up camp. Mashed finger & c.

4th. Stay in camp. Cook and knock around & c.
5th. Stay in camp. Cooked nice warm day.

6th. Bad night last night. Thunder & lightening powerful rain.
Fair day. Received orders at 9 o'clock at night to cook 3 days
rations & prepare to march at 7 o'clock in the morning.
Have cannon S.E. located from our camp.

On Saturday, February 1st, the battery picked a new campsite 3/4 of a mile from their previous camp and again erected chimneys for their tents. The actual move took place on Sunday, the next day. Once again, it was a bad day for moving; "cold, snowing & rainy." Why the men moved is not documented, but one possibility is that it was due to an unsanitary camp atmosphere.[10]

The next three days were boring and the men stayed in camp. On February 3rd, Peters mashed his finger while working around the camp. On the 5th, at least the weather warmed somewhat. Since Peters mentioned cooking several times, it would be interesting to have heard his exact menus.

On the night of February 6th the men were given orders to prepare enough rations for three days and be ready to march the next morning. Events to their west were rapidly coming to a head. On that morning Fort Henry, the sister fort to Fort Donelson had been attacked by Federal gunboats. With Fort Henry only twelve miles from Donelson, the Confederate defenders at Donelson would certainly have been able to hear the distant boom of the cannon. When Brig. Gen. Lloyd Tilghman, the Confederate commander at Henry, realized that the fort could not be successfully defended, he wisely ordered the infantry from the garrison to march immediately to Fort Donelson.

Gen. John Floyd had also received his marching orders. He was to transport his Virginia troops by train to Clarksville, Tennessee on the Cumberland River.[11]

Russellville, Logan Co, Kentucky
February 7th. Got up at 3 o'clock & prepared to march but could
not get transportation. Will have to wait until tomorrow.

8th. Put our guns on the cars & left R[ussellville] late in the evening
& traveled 5 Miles. Stayed all night in a house. Got up and went on.
[Last sentence marked through.]

Feb 9th. Got up this morning at 3 o'clock and started at daylight
traveled 30 miles to Clarksville. Lay upon the bank of river got
supper at hotel, paid 50c. Cold & frosty night.

While James and his battery waited again for transportation on February 7th, not far away a meeting was taking place that was determining the battery's meeting with destiny.

Back in Bowling Green, the town James and the battery had left only two weeks before, a meeting was called by Gen. Albert S. Johnston. Certainly the fall of Fort Henry and the seriousness of the situation was discussed. No details of this meeting have survived, but most likely Johnston decided that Ft. Donelson would be the focal point for a delaying action while Gen. Hardee and the main Confederate Army retreated past Nashville.[12] Regardless, Johnston put things in motion. The units from Russellville, Kentucky, consisting of Gen. Floyd's Brigade and that of Brig. Gen. Simon Bolivar Buckner were to converge with Brig. Gen. Gideon J. Pillow and his troops at Ft. Donelson. Brig. Gen. Bushrod R. Johnson was also ordered from Nashville to join the others at Donelson. Since John B. Floyd was the senior of these four brigadiers, he would assume overall command at the fort.

Once again James and the battery used the railroads to move the cannon and caissons, while he and the other soldiers took their horses and rode overland to reach their destination: Clarksville, Tennessee. The railroad that ran from Bowling Green, southwest through Russellville to Clarksville was the Memphis & Ohio Railroad. It continued in that same direction to Memphis. Another detachment of Confederate troops had already arrived at Clarksville and was making it secure. Clarksville must have been a busy military post. Gen. Pillow and his troops who were now stationed there had turned it into the "...most efficient supply post on the Cumberland River."[13]

At least James was able to purchase a good hot meal at the local hotel for fifty cents the evening of his arrival.

> *Clarksville, Tennessee*
> *February 10. Got up this morning at daylight went up in town.*
> *Got breakfast at private house. Clever people friendly. I put our*
> *horses on boat crossed river and went to camp about 1 mile from*
> *river. Got a letter from home.*
>
> *11th. Got order to prepare to march. Made preparations but could*
> *not get transportation.*
>
> *12th. Stay about camp waiting for transportation. Started sunset*
> *traveled all night to Cumberland City. Arrived there at day break.*

The advantages of being near a friendly, sympathetic southern city were again demonstrated as James noted he was able to get a breakfast at a private house "...up in town." After breakfast, James and his compatriots found a boat that would take them and their horses across the Cumberland River. That same day James received his second letter from home.

Probably while at Clarksville, but maybe even as far back as Russellville, James and the battery met up again with the battery of John Henry Guy (the Goochland Artillery.) Guy also kept a journal and wrote about the build-up to Ft. Donelson and the events that occurred there. Even though Guy wrote the journal a few months after the fact, he adds some vital details about this period of time.[14] We will therefore also reference some of his diary entries to supplement the brief account of James Peters.

As James and his comrades went into camp the generals were again discussing strategy. This time Generals Floyd and Buckner wanted to concentrate their delaying forces not at Fort Donelson but at Cumberland City, Tennessee.[15] Their reasoning appears to have been that a small force at the fort could hold the Union Army's atten-

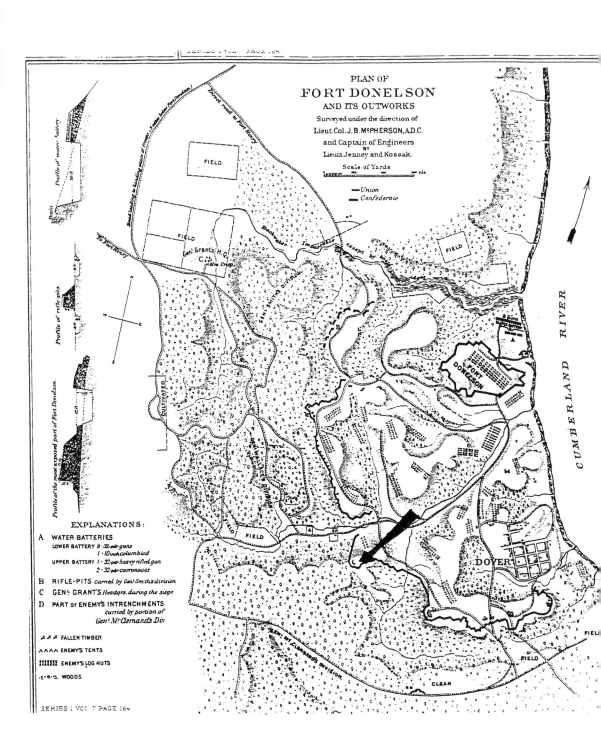

Map of Fort Donelson and town of Dover from Official Records Atlas. Arrow points to position of French's Battery.

tion, while the troops at Cumberland City could move against the Union's lines of communication. It was as a result of this strategy that on February 11 Floyd ordered the part of his brigade that was encamped at Clarksville to move down to Cumberland City. James and the men broke camp and got their supplies and horses together, only to once again wait on railroad transportation. Finally at sunset on the next day, James and the men loaded the cannon and caissons on the railcars of the Memphis & Ohio Railroad. Also on the same train were the cannon and some of the men from John Henry Guy's Battery. James and some of his comrades, along with Guy and some of his men traveled all night by horseback to Cumberland City, arriving about daybreak on the 13th. Guy stated that the guns and the rest of the men that had traveled by train arrived there first.[16]

At Cumberland City activity must have been frantic. A short time after James and his battery arrived, orders were given that the key defensive position would not be Cumberland City but Fort Donelson. Major George A. Cunningham, of the 51st Virginia Infantry, was commanding the artillery battalion that included French's Battery. Cunningham, who answered to Gen. Floyd, ordered that the rifled piece belonging to French's Battery be left at Cumberland. The reason given was that the battery did not have the special ammunition required for a rifled cannon.[17] (Cunningham would later command all the artillery at Fort Donelson.) This left the battery with three cannon, probably all smoothbore. French's and Guy's Batteries and the other Virginia troops at Cumberland were ordered immediately to move on to Fort Donelson.

Meanwhile a little-known Union general named Ulysses S. Grant and his army were moving from Fort Henry toward Fort Donelson. Anticipating the inevitable attack, the defenders were digging additional rifle pits and cutting trees and saplings for abatis.

The remainder of the twenty-odd mile trip from Cumberland City to the fort would be by steamboat, as the Memphis & Ohio Railroad turned southwest, away from the river. By this time, there were only two steamboats available to the Confederates on the Cumberland River, the *General Anderson* and the *May Duke*.[18]

Dover, Tennessee
February 13. Left Cumberland City & camp to this place &
went 1 mile from river & stopped & commenced throwing up
breastworks cold & snowing.

Exactly when James Peters and the other members of French's Battery boarded their boat and landed at the little crossroads of Dover, Tennessee is vague. Dover served as the wharf and landing for Fort Donelson where troops and supplies were unloaded.

Most sources agree that Gen. Floyd and at least some of his troops landed at the Dover wharf near daylight on Thursday, February 13.[19] This placed Floyd at the Fort in time for breakfast with Gen. Pillow. John H. Guy, on the other hand, stated that "...we got to Ft. Donelson about noon on the same day [Thursday]."[20] (Most available sources do agree that Guy's and French's Batteries arrived on the same boat.) Napoleon French and others have stated that the battery did not arrive until the evening of the 13th.[21] Capt. French, however, was not actually present at Donelson, having once again been left back due to illness, and his report was written using second-hand infor-

Organization of Confederate Forces
Fort Donelson, Tennessee
February, 1862

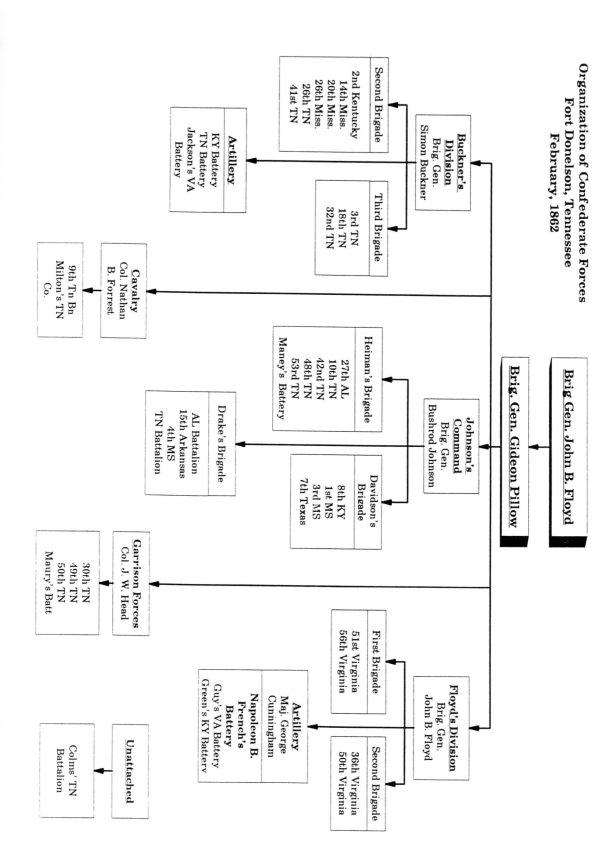

Brig. Gen. John B. Floyd

Brig. Gen. Gideon Pillow

Buckner's Division
Brig. Gen. Simon Buckner

Second Brigade
2nd Kentucky
14th Miss.
20th Miss.
26th Miss.
26th TN
41st TN

Third Brigade
3rd TN
18th TN
32nd TN

Artillery
KY Battery
TN Battery
Jackson's VA Battery

Cavalry
Col. Nathan B. Forrest
9th Tn Bn
Milton's TN Co.

Johnson's Command
Brig. Gen. Bushrod Johnson

Heiman's Brigade
27th AL
10th TN
42nd TN
48th TN
53rd TN
Maney's Battery

Drake's Brigade
AL Battalion
15th Arkansas
4th MS
TN Battalion

Davidson's Brigade
8th KY
1st MS
3rd MS
7th Texas

Garrison Forces
Col. J. W. Head
30th TN
49th TN
50th TN
Maury's Batt.

Floyd's Division
Brig. Gen. John B. Floyd

First Brigade
51st Virginia
56th Virginia

Second Brigade
36th Virginia
50th Virginia

Artillery
Maj. George Cunningham
Napoleon B. French's Battery
Guy's VA Battery
Green's KY Battery

Unattached
Colns' TN Battalion

- 36 -

mation. Given that James' last diary entry agrees with Guy's that they arrived at Cumberland City at daylight on the 13th, then about noon seems to be the most logical arrival time at Dover. It is likely that the two steamboats made multiple trips to ferry the men, cannon, and horses, and that Floyd may indeed have arrived on one of the first shuttle runs, while James and the battery arrived on a later run.

When the last of Floyd's Virginians arrived at Dover, his brigade totaled between 1,200 and 1,400 men. The brigade consisted of:

> 51st Virginia Infantry
> 56th Virginia Infantry
> 36th Virginia Infantry (Col. McCausland)
> 50th Virginia Infantry
> French's Battery (Lt. Maitland)
> Guy's Battery (Capt. Guy)
> Green's Kentucky Battery

With the arrival of the last Confederate forces at Fort Donelson the strength of the garrison stood at about 15,000 men.

When French's Battery arrived at Fort Donelson, it was immediately assigned engineering duty building more breastworks. If James had any time to observe his overall surroundings and position, he would probably have sized up the large fort this way:

> Fort Donelson, an earthen fort like Fort Henry, stood atop a hill about a
> hundred feet above the waters of the Cumberland River. Two water
> batteries, called the Upper and Lower, according to the river flow, mounted
> 12 heavy seacoast guns, some of which had been shipped from Virginia...[22]

These heavy seacoast guns consisted of one 6.5-inch rifled piece, a 10-inch Columbiad and a main line of 32-pound cannon. Additionally:

> ...the ascents, seventy or eighty feet in height, up which a foe must charge,
> and that, where they were weakest, they were strengthened by trees felled
> outwardly in front of them, so that the interlacing limbs and branches
> seemed impassable by men under fire. At points inside the outworks, on
> the inner slopes of the hills, defended thus from view of an enemy as well
> as from his shot, lay the huts and loghouses of the garrison.[23]

John H. Guy described it thusly: "...the fort made of dirt & with only a tolerable armament of guns, was near the river & commanded it; our lines began at the fort & ran a little out from the river & then up the River."[24]

By evening, French's Battery had been ordered into position in the defensive line. It was placed on the east side of Erin Hollow, a ravine that was defended on the opposite side by the four-gun battery of Capt. Frank Maney from Tennessee. Providing infantry support to them were the 4th Mississippi and the 15th Arkansas Regiments from Col. Joseph Drake's Brigade.[25] By this time, Guy's Battery had been sent to another part of the defenses. It is possible, even though James Peters made no mention

Right Wing.   Schwartz's Battery.   Taylor's Battery.   Battery, Rifle

of it, that French's Battery saw its first action on Thursday.[26] It is more likely, however, that their first exchange occurred on the next day (Friday).

By nightfall, the Union Army had the fort almost completely surrounded, except for the river side of the fort. There had been a few probing attacks against the fort's defenses, but the major engagement would come later. Maney's Battery had seen sharp action against one of these attacks, and had successfully defended its position.

James noted again the weather as being "cold and snowing." That would have been the weather conditions by nightfall, as the morning had been calm and almost spring-like. The temperature had dropped as the day wore on, with a cold rain falling

ery.   Rifle Pits. Water Battery.   Fort Donelson.   General Smith's Charge, Iowa Second.

and turning to sleet before dark. Overnight the temperature dipped to 12 degrees.[27] The men of the Virginia artillery batteries must have spent a terrible night, huddled in their blankets. Their tents were probably left back at Cumberland City with their baggage.

Friday, February 14, St. Valentine's Day, dawned with bitter cold. Some snow had also fallen on the men in the fort during the night. Some of the men in the lower water battery said they had seldom felt a more piercing wind than blew that morning.

While James and his comrades fought for their lives at Fort Donelson, the Confederate forces that remained behind quietly abandoned Bowling Green, Kentucky and headed south.[28]

Attack of the Union gunboats on the water batteries at Fort Donelson. *Harper's Weekly*

Position of Taylor and McCallister's Union Batteries during the Battle of Fort Donelson. James Peters and French's Battery dueled with this battery. *Harper's Weekly*

Lower Battery—9 Guns.   Upper Battery—8 Guns.   The Fort proper,

14th. Fought all day from breastwork. Heavy fight at fort with gunboats. Got one man killed by shell. Cold, frozen weather. Suffer greatly.

There was some action at the point in the defenses where French's Battery was stationed during the morning of the 14th, but the major threat planned by the Union forces for that day would come by water. Union Flag Officer Andrew Foote, commanding the same flotilla of gunboats that had forced Fort Henry to surrender only a week before, was now in position on the Cumberland River to do the same thing to Fort Donelson. Because of all the preparations aboard the gunboats, they did not get under way toward the fort until around 2:00 p.m.[29] The duel began when the flotilla was more than a mile away with the Confederate water battery opening fire with its long-range 6.5 inch rifled gun. By the time the Union ships were within about 400 yards of the water batteries, the shelling from both sides was intense. By 3:30 or 4:00 p.m. several of the Union ships had been damaged and floated aimlessly in the river, and the others were ordered to retreat. Cheers went up from the Confederate lines. The defenders of Fort Donelson had shown Gen. Grant that their defenses would not be taken by gunboats on the river.

Sometime after the gunboats retreated, James and his comrades of French's Battery launched a bombardment on Union batteries opposite their position. These Union batteries were Battery D of the 1st Illinois Light Artillery, commanded by Capt. Edward McAllister and Battery H of the 1st Missouri Light Artillery, commanded by Capt. F. Welker. McAllister had at least one 24-pound cannon in his battery and Welker's Battery was equipped with Parrott Rifles. French's Battery was firing not only solid or exploding shells, but canister from their smoothbores. Canister consisted of a tin can filled with musket balls that in essence turned the cannon into a large shotgun which was effective up to about 200 yards. Maney's Battery joined in the shelling with French's Battery. One of Welker's guns was silenced when "...one nearly direct hit mangled one soldier horribly and sent his compatriots into the brush."[30] It was probably during this artillery duel that the member of French's Battery James Peters mentioned was killed by an enemy shell. He was Pvt. William H. Oney, who enlisted with James at the Alvis Farm back in Mercer County.[31] This shelling from French's and Maney's Batteries may have been in support of a Confederate attack ordered on the Union right flank. Gen. Floyd recalled this attack, probably due to the late hour. The men of French's Battery had experienced their baptismal of fire.

By evening sleet and then snow began falling in substantial amounts, prompting Peters' comment that the men did "suffer greatly." John Henry Guy, whose battery was stationed in another part of the works, later stated that "The cold was so great all day & the night following, that the men suffered more from it than they had done since they had been in the service."[32]

That night, the four Confederate generals realized the Union forces surrounding the fort had been steadily reinforced and now had the Confederates outnumbered almost two-to-one. They settled on a desperate plan for the next morning: attempt to cut their way out of the Union encirclement.

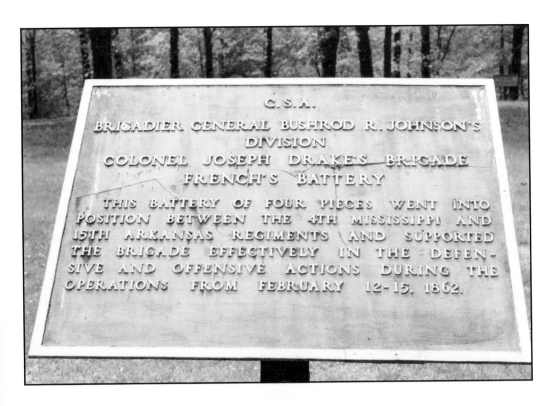

C.S.A.

BRIGADIER GENERAL BUSHROD R. JOHNSON'S
DIVISION
COLONEL JOSEPH DRAKE'S BRIGADE
FRENCH'S BATTERY

THIS BATTERY OF FOUR PIECES WENT INTO
POSITION BETWEEN THE 4TH MISSISSIPPI AND
15TH ARKANSAS REGIMENTS AND SUPPORTED
THE BRIGADE EFFECTIVELY IN THE DEFEN-
SIVE AND OFFENSIVE ACTIONS DURING THE
OPERATIONS FROM FEBRUARY 12-15, 1862.

Position of French's Battery, Fort Donelson National Military Park.

15th. Heavy fighting commenced at daylight on our left.
Ordered battery on our right. Fought from 11 until 12 o'clock.
Went to camp to get dinner was ordered back to breastwork.
Kept there until night. Heavy fight on our right. Fight ceased
at night by repulsing the enemy.

As Saturday, February 15 dawned on a frozen and snowy landscape once again, the Confederate forces amassed in Erin Hollow for the attack out of the breastworks against the Union forces. This bold move, the high command hoped, would open the road toward Charlotte and allow the encircled army to escape. By six a.m. the Confederate attack got under way, with French's and the other artillery batteries in that area providing heavy fire. By eight a.m. the fighting had moved out to the Wynn's Ferry Road, and the Confederate batteries, including French's, continued to fire for support.

James Peters added the brief but important sentence in his diary: "Ordered battery on our right." This sentence has left us guessing exactly which battery he was referring to. It could have referred to Frank Maney's Battery.[33] Joining Maney's Battery the previous night was the Tennessee battery of Capt. Parker.[34] Peters could have been referring to this unit, possibly, as we know Parker was wounded sometime that day. Perhaps more important is the simple inferred fact that Peters was trusted enough by either Lt. Maitland or another officer to put him in charge of additional cannon. James must have mastered the soldier's craft well.

After this initial thrust by the Confederates, Gen. Buckner decided to seize the opportunity to attack the angle created in the Union line by the initial onslaught. All the available artillery batteries in the area were ordered to concentrate their fire on the flanks and rear of the Union position. This included Graves', Maney's, Guy's and French's Batteries. This firing is what James Peters referred to as his fighting between 11 a.m. and 12 noon. The Confederate guns were delivering mostly grape-shot and canister. It was during this one-hour period that French's Battery dueled with Capt. Edward McAllister's Battery D, 1st Illinois Light Artillery. McAllister's Battery had been raining fire on the attacking Confederate infantry regiments. Union reports stated that one shot from the Rebel guns passed through three horses, and damaged two of the Union guns. McAllister reported four killed and several wounded, and the Union infantry regiments in that area were forced to seek cover in a ravine.[35] McAllister's men were forced to retreat and left two of their pieces mired or tangled in the brush. The entire Union force in that part of the battlefield was being forced to retreat. "The dike was leaking and no one had enough fingers to stem the tide."[36]

All the Confederate batteries had remained in their defensive positions supporting the attack, except Graves', which was ordered forward out of its defensive position. The Union guns, however, spotted this movement and Graves and his two guns were sent retreating back toward the defenses.

By noon the Confederates had succeeded with the first phase of their plan: the road was cleared and the escape path for the Confederate Army at Donelson lay wide open!

The opportunity was short-lived. Indecision seemed to overtake the four Confed-

Site of French's Battery at Fort Donelson. Erin Hollow is in back of the cannon on the left.

Some of the Confederate trenches still visible at Fort Donelson National Military Park.

erate generals. General Pillow ordered a retreat of part of the attacking force. General Buckner expressed his readiness to act as rear guard if the army evacuated the works by the now open roads. General Floyd, being in overall command, vacillated. In their defense, it must be said that many Union regiments were rallying and being reinforced while the attacking Confederate infantry and cavalry were becoming very tired. General Ulysses Grant returned to the battlefield after a meeting on one of the gunboats with Admiral Foote and began to pull his command back together. Gen. Floyd, believing that a Federal assault was in the making, finally ordered the Confederates back to the defenses.

Grant and his generals now saw an opportunity to regain some of their lost ground. Their counterattack began in the early afternoon. One of the Union brigades facing French's Battery was commanded by Gen. Lew Wallace. By mid-afternoon, French's Battery was exchanging artillery fire with the battery commanded by Capt. Jasper M. Dresser. This unit was Battery A of the Illinois Light Artillery. Dresser eventually limbered his guns and retreated.[37] This incident is supported by a recording of the events in the Compiled Service Records of French's Battery: "Assisted in the fight of Saturday morning and had a light engagement in the afternoon with a Federal battery which lasted about 20 minutes when we silenced it and caused it to remove from its position." French's Battery commanded by Lt. Maitland along with Maney's Battery continued to fire on the Union forces. Between four and five p.m., Col. Charles Cruft, commanding one of the Union brigades of the Third Division, came under the grapeshot and shell fire from French's Battery. This afternoon battle against the counterattacking Union forces constituted James' comment of "heavy fight on our right."

As night fell, the firing stopped. James' entry that they had repulsed the enemy was only partially true. True, the Confederates had virtually stopped the Union counterattack. In the front of French's Battery, the positions were the same as at dawn so it would have appeared to James Peters and his comrades of the battery that they had successfully repulsed the enemy. Indeed, many of the Union regiments had been ordered to withdraw and dig-in. The Federals, however, at one point had pierced the earthworks of Fort Donelson. "Night found the two armies almost where they had been in the morning, except that [Union General Charles] Smith had cracked the outer perimeter."[38] Lt. Maitland and James Conrad Peters could be justifiably proud of the efforts of their battery that day. They had stood head-to-head with the Union infantry and artillery and had won over both.

By dark a heavy snow squall materialized and the evening and night promised to be the coldest yet.[39]

As the Confederate soldiers in the defenses shivered under blankets, coats, or any other cover they could find, the generals were once again making drastic decisions that would seal the fate of the common soldiers at Fort Donelson.

Confederate scouts were sent out into the night to determine the Federal positions. Conflicting reports came back that the Federals had strengthened or at least held their previous position on the Confederate left. Gen. Buckner stated that his men were starving and tired and could not hold out against another attack in the morning. Gen. Pillow argued to hold out another day. Gen. Johnson still favored a night-time withdrawal. By midnight, opinions still leaned toward evacuation and escape. By 1:00 a.m., the evacuation schedule was set for daybreak, which was about 5:30. Soon after this, however, scouts returned with the intelligence that the Forge Road was in the possession of the Federals. Col. Nathan Bedford Forrest, in command of most of the cavalry at Fort Donelson, was skeptical of these reports and sent out his own scouts. His men determined that some of the roads were now also flooded by backwater. Medical authorities stated that an attempt to escape by the flooded roads on such a cold night would endanger the health of the soldiers. It was decided that the attempted evacuation would cost too many lives. Gen. Floyd was ready to give up and surrender was being discussed. Nathan Bedford Forrest quickly took his 800 cavalrymen and a few infantrymen and headed across the flooded roads. He would be praised for making good his escape. The next discussion was one that would "live in infamy." Floyd stated that he feared for his life if captured due to his pre-war role as U.S. Secretary of War. Pillow also stated he feared of falling into enemy hands. Only Buckner appeared willing to stay behind and negotiate a surrender. Floyd then turned over command to Gen. Pillow, and Pillow immediately passed it down to Buckner. Floyd was promised time to get as many of his men out of Donelson as possible on the steamboats.[40]

John Henry Guy related in his journal incidents which occurred among Floyd's troops, including Guy's and French's Batteries:

> Just before daylight I was awaked a 3rd time with new orders to bring my men instantly to the River, leaving guns horses and everything and informed that unless they hurried there in the greatest haste they would be left by the steamboat, which was then ready to start and had on board most of Floyd's Brigade. I instantly awoke the men and took them to the River, but the steamboat had already left the landing when we got there, and just never returned to the landing, though Genl. Floyd who was on board seemed for awhile disposed to cause it to do so, but he was finally deterred by the great crowd that had now collected in great disorder on the bank under the apprehension that rushing on board they might sink the boat.[41]

The boat Guy referred to was the *Gen. Anderson*, although there was a second and smaller ship (probably the *May Duke*) used in the evacuation. Floyd ordered Major William N. Brown of the 20th Mississippi to guard the approach to the steamboat landing and to prevent any stragglers, who were not of Floyd's Brigade, from rushing aboard the steamboat. Brown stated in his report: "The boats being detained until nearly daylight and the news of a surrender spreading through the camp, caused many to flock to the river, almost panic-stricken and frantic, to make good their escape by getting aboard."[42] The boats made their first trip across the river to safety just before daybreak. As the boats returned to the wharf, Gen. Buckner warned Floyd that unless the boats at the dock departed immediately, Buckner would order them shelled, as the surrender was taking place. Quickly Gen. Floyd, along with Col. John McCausland and his Virginia infantry made it aboard and the *Gen. Anderson* pulled rapidly away from the Dover wharf. Exactly how many men escaped with Floyd is not known, but estimates go as high as 1,500 men. James Peters recounted the activities of that day by these entries:

> *16th. Enemy reinforced by 12:00. Commenced retreat at daylight*

went to river but could not get transportation & surrendered ourselves
prisoners of war. Stay at river until dark. Put on board a boat to be
sent to Cairo very well treated. Bad cold weather, rainy and snowing,
muddy.

This reinforcement of the enemy "...by 12:00" meant that the Federals had solidified their positions by midnight.

It must have been pandemonium at the wharf as French's and Guy's Batteries gathered along with the infantry regiments that had heard the rumors of surrender and possible escape via the river. John Henry Guy remembered that morning this way:

As soon as thoughts of escape were abandoned the soldiers, or such of them as were near the river and they were there to the number of several thousand, gave themselves up to breaking open boxes and barrels of Army stores, which lay in great quantity about the steamboat landing, and appropriating the contents. There were many barrels of sugar, whiskey and crackers, and hogsheads of molasses and they were drunk and eaten freely.[43]

The joy was short-lived, as white flags of surrender began to appear. Gen. Buckner had earlier sent an aide to Grant proposing commissioners to agree on the terms of surrender. Grant had sent back the answer that would make him famous:

"... no terms except <u>unconditional surrender</u>."

Federal troops marched down to the wharf and drew up around the Confederates as the surrendering troops stacked their arms. The remainder of the day was taken up with arrangements between the generals and by nightfall Federal ships had pulled in to the wharf to begin loading the prisoners. James Peters stated he and his men waited at the river in terrible weather until the boats arrived: "Bad cold weather, rainy and snowing, muddy."

As James Peters and the men of French's Battery boarded the boat under the watchful eye of the Federal guards, their thoughts must have turned to what the future would bring. They had braved the weather and the Federal attacks for four days at Fort Donelson. The battery had been victorious or at least held their own against the Federals, only to be surrendered by a general who fled to escape capture.

The men of the artillery batteries from Virginia would now face a fate as deadly as the Battle of Fort Donelson; they would become prisoners of war in a northern prison camp.

Reconstructed upper water battery, Fort Donelson National Military Park.

Restored Dover Tavern and Hotel, Fort Donelson National Military Park. Confederate forces surrendered to Gen. Ulysses Grant here, Feb. 1862.

RICHMOND, *Virginia., March 11, 1862.*

Hon. J.P. BENJAMIN,
Secretary of War, Richmond, Virginia.:

SIR: The reports of Brigadier-Generals Floyd and Pillow of the defense and fall of Fort Donelson are unsatisfactory. I can but hope that explanations may be made which will change the aspect given to the affair by their statements.

In the mean time you will order General A. S. Johnston to relieve both of those officers from command, and to indicate to them that information is wanted as to their failure to give timely notice of the insufficiency of the garrison to repel the attack and their failure to attempt to save the army by evacuating the post when it was found to be untenable, and especially why they abandoned the command and by what means their escape was effected; further, to state upon what principle was a selection made of particular troops, being certain regiments of the senior general's brigade, to whose use the transportation on hand should be appropriated.

Copies of the reports received will be furnished to me for transmission to Congress.

Very respectfully, yours,

JEFFERSON DAVIS. [44]

Chapter VI
Life as a POW

The number of Confederate soldiers who surrendered to Union forces that fateful Sunday is unknown. Since the garrison strength at the fort before the battle was approximately 15,000, then about 12,000 probably surrendered. Some Union reports were inflated to state that the garrison was almost 21,000 strong and that almost 15,000 surrendered. This was based on the report of the Union commissary officer at Cairo, Illinois who stated he furnished 14,623 rations to the prisoners as they passed by Cairo on their way north.[1] Confederate casualties appear to have been less than 1,000 killed and wounded. This added to the approximately 800 who escaped with Col. Forrest and the 1,500 men who escaped on the boats with Gen. Floyd points to about 12,000 men surrendered as accurate. In French's Battery the number of men who surrendered with James Conrad Peters was well documented. The adjutant of French's Battery wrote: "The surrender took place on Sunday morning when 42 men and 3 commissioned officers (Lieut's) with one servant were captured."[2]

The Confederate prisoners spent that Sunday night huddled on board the boats at the Dover wharf. John Henry Guy recalled: "On Monday [Feburary 17] the Federals had got together enough transports to take off all the prisoners & we started to St. Louis."[3] The next four days were occupied with sailing down the Cumberland to where it joins the Ohio River at Smithland, Kentucky, then west down the Ohio to where it meets the Mississippi at Cairo, Illinois. At Cairo they turned north and sailed up the Mississippi to St. Louis. Even this boat trip was not without its perils. As word spread of the nature of the human cargo being transported, the boats were fired upon from shore. At various points along the way several prisoners were wounded from these gunshots.

These four days no doubt gave the men time to reflect on the surrender, the reasons for it, and what they faced in the North. John H. Guy stated in his journal: "Of one thing however I am certain, & that is that the surrender was unnecessary and shameful. Of this opinion are all officers & soldiers of the army that I have heard speak of it."[4] It was obvious that the men felt betrayed by their commanding officers. Floyd in particular would receive the lion's share of the blame. The Comte de Paris wrote after the War: "The Confederates did wrong to reward the criminal services Mr. Floyd had rendered them whilst Secretary of war in Washington by entrusting him with important military commands; they paid dear for this error."[5] Others were more lenient with him: "Floyd, however, was more to be pitied than censured. He was not a trained soldier....He had not the least familiarity with the task of holding a fortified position like Ft. Donelson, and he undertook its defense reluctantly."[6] Floyd tried to rationalize his actions this way: "I presume the general [Albert S. Johnston] knew, before I was ordered to Fort Donelson, that neither the works nor the troops sent there could withstand the force which he knew the enemy had in hand and which could be brought speedily to that point."[7] Gen. John Floyd would never hold another important field command in the Confederate Army. He was instead put in charge of the state troops in southwestern Virginia. His health deteriorated and he died at Abingdon

CONSTRUCTION OF FLOATING MORTAR BATTERIES BY THE FEDERAL GOVERNMENT A
the capture of Fort Sumter Commander John Rodgers was summonned to Washington, and to him wa
assumed the expense and supervision, but in the autumn of 1861 the matter was transferred to the Nav
brought to take part in the capture of Forts Henry and Donaldson. From a sketch by H. Lovie.

Wharf at St. Louis, Mo. Frank Leslie's *Illustrated* Newspaper

ERRY, ST. LOUIS, MO.—The importance of a navy on our Western rivers was early appreciated. A month after
of creating such a navy. In the early stages of the undertaking the War Department under Secretary Cameron
e iron-clad gunboats and thirty-eight mortar-boats were hastily constructed at St. Louis, and in February, 1862, were

on Aug. 26, 1863. He would be remembered as "the typical nineteenth-century political general whose ambitions exceeded his military talents to the detriment of the Confederacy."[8]

At least there was a small ray of sunshine for the tired and hungry Confederate soldiers as the boats docked at the St. Louis wharf. The townspeople turned out and demonstrated a very humane act. Pvt. T. J. Moore of the 3rd Tennessee recounted this welcome: "The good people of that city [St. Louis] brought us wagon loads of good things to eat."[9] Some of the local women also passed tobacco to the prisoners. While stopped at St. Louis the men and officers were separated, with the officers being sent to Camp Chase at Columbus, Ohio. Some of the privates were sent to a prison at Indianapolis. The majority, including James Peters, would continue on north. After staying overnight at St. Louis, the flotilla traveled upriver a few miles to the rail center at Alton, Illinois. There the prisoners were herded onto railroad cars of the Illinois Central Railroad and the train headed north.

> *Chicago, Illinois   Camp Douglas*
> *February 24th 1862. Arrived here yesterday from Ft. Donelson.*
> *Traveled from Fort D. 4 days by water to St. Louis & to Chicago*
> *by railway had hard time of it.*

So exactly a week to the day from the surrender at Fort Donelson, approximately 4,500 tired and sick Confederate prisoners arrived at their destination. According to Private T. J. Moore, after the men unloaded at the train station, they had to march the last three miles "...through the mud and slush...to Camp Douglas."[10] It would certainly not be the last mud and slush they would see in their new surroundings near Chicago. Monday, Feb. 24th, was the first time since his capture that James Peters had an opportunity to write in his journal. His remark "had hard time of it" is certainly understandable. During the week aboard the boats and freight cars, many of the men had become sick with various illnesses. Sickness and disease would become a part of daily life at Camp Douglas.

Camp Douglas had certainly not been originally constructed as a prison camp. Like similar camps throughout the north, Douglas had been built as a muster camp for Union troops. When the word came that several thousand Confederate prisoners were being brought to this camp, several modifications were instituted. The sites in the north such as Chicago, Elmira, New York and Point Lookout, Maryland were chosen because distant prison sites supposedly would discourage escape attempts. About the time of James Peters' arrival at Douglas, it was described thusly:

> The camp consisted of three miles of 14 foot high fence with the usual gates, sentries, dead-lines, observation towers and barracks. The latter were mostly one story affairs of wood each with three tiers of bunks for 125 to 150 men.[11]

The high wood fence mentioned had probably not been completed by the day of James' arrival. This was the Union's first experience in collecting and transporting Confederates to prison camps in such large numbers, and the men of Camp Douglas would suffer while the bugs were worked out of the system.

2nd March. Have been sick all this week nearly. Have plenty to eat
well treated.

Sunday March 9th. Been very unwell this week. Had the jaundice
moved our quarters to the old church last week 3 co's in it Jackson's
Artillery, Guys and French's.

James was sick with the jaundice during this first week of March. Today we generally think of jaundice as a disease affecting the liver. During the Civil War, however, the term was applied to a general yellowness of the eyes, skin, and urine and accompanied by constipation, loss of appetite and general lassitude. James and the other members of the Virginia artillery units were moved to an old church. This was probably the chapel that had been built at Camp Douglas by the YMCA in 1861.[12] This chapel was a point of controversy during March of 1862. The YMCA complained that the prisoners were being deprived of their place of worship because the chapel was being used as a barracks. During these months, it was also used as a hospital for the sick prisoners. At least James and his compatriots could talk again to their friends in Guy's Battery whom they had fought beside at Fort Donelson.

Camp Douglas   Chicago Illinois
March 16th 1862. Have got about well I think. Thank God for it
for it is bad to be sick here.

James' complete understatement that "...it is bad to be sick here" was certainly true. Once a contagious disease started in the prison camps, it spread like wildfire. The lack of sanitary procedures and presence of open latrines accelerated other virus-borne ailments. One in eight died of pneumonia, pleurisy, colds, or bowel disorders and in March of 1862 the number of prisoners in the camp hospital rose to 325.[13] To make matters worse, three of the Confederate surgeons refused to work because they said they would not take orders from a Federal officer. This was soon rectified when they were threatened with being confined to the dungeon in irons. Two of James' compatriots from French's Battery who had enlisted with him at the Alvis Farm died at Camp Douglas in March: Pvt. John Comer and Pvt. John Fisher. They were only two out of 125 men who died there during March.

March 31st. Nothing of interest has occurred up to this time.
I have been well. Had preaching once a day. We have been
well treated. Furnished books treats & c by the preachers.
Move last week from church to barracks again. Has been
tolerable bad weather plenty to eat of bacon, pork and beef,
light bread beans & c.

Rev. Edmund Tuttle and his fellow preachers worked hard to supply the spiritual needs of the prisoners. They furnished not only Bibles but also the small "tracts" which were probably the books referred to here by James. During the month of March, James and

THE WAR IN THE WEST—BIRD'S-EYE VIEW OF CAMP DOUGLAS, CHICAGO, ILL.,

APRIL

View of Camp Douglas prison camp near Chicago, Ill., made on April 26, 1862, soon after James and his fellow POWs arrived. The prison barracks are the long row of buildings at right of layout, just inside the stockade fence. Courtesy Chicago Historical Society

ETENTION OF REBEL PRISONERS.—FROM A SKETCH BY MR. F. MUNSON, OF CHICAGO

his compatriots were moved from the chapel back to the barracks. This was due to Col. William Hoffman (the Union Commissary General of Prisoners) ordering the camp commander, Col. James Mulligan, to remove the resident prisoners and allow the building to be returned to the control of the YMCA. At this point, at least, the food was still being delivered in good ration. Here we get a good insight into James' diet, with his mention of both pork and beef, as well as bread and beans "& c" being in the prisoners' diet.

> *Camp Douglas   Chicago Ill*
> *April 5th 1862. I am still in good health & spirits. Thank*
> *the Lord for it. Nothing unusual has occurred this week.*
> *Rainy & muddy weather. No prospect of being released*
> *that I can see.*

James was thankful for his good health and spirits after his sickness in March. The bad weather continued. James' remark of "no prospect of being released..." was a natural one. Primary in every prisoners mind, after mere survival of course, was the idea of either being released or the possibility of escape. Ten prisoners had escaped during the first week of April, and when they were recaptured, Col. Mulligan had them parade around the prison with boards tied on their backs reading: "Escaped Prisoners Recaptured."

> *[April] 19th. Nothing out of ordinary line of camp life has*
> *occurred up to this date. I have been well except toothache. Has*
> *been rainy weather & very muddy. We have nothing to do but*
> *cook & eat & wash our clothes & read & sleep.*

The drudgery of prison life is shown here in James' comment that they had nothing to do but cook, eat, wash clothes, read and sleep. A study of a calendar for 1862 shows that James wrote most of his diary entries on the weekends, as Mar. 9 & 16 were Sundays, and April 5 & 19th were Saturdays.

> *Camp Douglas May 6th 1862*
> *I am still well & hearty. Nothing of importance has occurred*
> *up to this date It is nice weather now.*
>
> *May 12th. It has been fine weather this week.*
> *I have been well this week except a bad cough & a sore arm*
> *from vaccination.*

At last by mid-May the bad weather appears to have ended. James commented that the weather had been fine through May 12. The vaccination James referred to was most likely for smallpox as this type of inoculation began at the camp during April. Smallpox was a huge problem at Camp Douglas, and a quarantine hospital, known as the "Smallpox Hospital," was established. Dr. A. M. Clark, the Medical Inspector, was convinced he could contain the smallpox through vaccinations. In reality, many avoided the vaccinations because some of the infections which resulted were considered worse than the disease itself.[14]

> *May 29th 1862. It has been cool harsh weather for the*
> *last few days. Got a letter from home which gave me great*
> *satisfaction. I have been well except toothache.*

Once again the Chicago weather turned harsh on the prisoners at Camp Douglas. After being confined for three months, James received his first letter from home. The letter from home which gave James "great satisfaction" could have informed him that his wife, Polly Ann would soon give birth to their second child.

> *Camp Douglas Sunday June 1st 1862.*
> *It is very cool & wet this morning . I have had a very bad*
> *swollen jaw from the toothache. I feel well this morning &*
> *oh, I could be so happy if I was at home with my wife and*
> *child.*

James still suffered from the toothache that he first reported in his journal on April 19th. One of the few moments of homesickness that James recorded while away from his family is recorded in this entry. He had now survived the horrors of Camp Douglas for over three months and his thoughts frequently turned to his family back in Mercer County.

> *June 8th Sunday. It has been very cool damp weather this*
> *week. Have been well. It is fine weather now.*

The next day, Monday June 9, 1862, was a special day for James and his family. On Monday, Sarah Emeline Peters was born to James and Polly Ann. We do not know how long it took word of the event to reach James, but it was undoubtedly several days if not weeks.

> *Camp Douglas June 22nd 1862 Sunday.*
> *It has been very cool weather for the past 2 weeks.*
> *Nothing unusual has occurred in the past 2 weeks.*
> *I have been well.*
>
> *June 27th. Received a letter from father this week which gave*
> *me great satisfaction. We were all ordered on the square*
> *& our barracks searched and our packs, knives taken was*
> *of any size. & two men --.*

The letter from Christian S. Peters, James' father, probably brought the news of Sarah Emeline Peters' birth, although James does not state that specifically, only that the letter gave him "...great satisfaction." Both mother and daughter were doing well. The incident James recounts of the men being turned out of their barracks, and articles being confiscated occurred on Monday, June 23, 1862. The camp had just been turned over to a new Union commander, Col. Joseph H. Tucker. Tucker had been residing there, recruiting a new regiment of troops. Tucker must have been convinced that there were too many weapons among the prisoners and that this was a security problem. He probably also wanted to show his newly acquired authority. Prior to Tucker's administration, prisoners had been allowed to keep small pocket knives and certain other utensils. Tucker brought in the Chicago police for a massive shakedown. The prisoners, of course, thought that using the Chicago police was unfair, and the policemen were accused of pocketing not only various confiscated items but money and other personal items as well.[15]

> *Camp Douglas Sunday July 6th.*
> *I have been well. Received a letter from uncle Zenas Hanley.*
> *33 gun salute for 4th of July. Excitement in camp very warm*
> *weather & dry. Wrote letter to home Monday.*

The uncle Zenas Hanley that James referred to had married his mother's sister, Emeline Karnes. (James' mother was Mary Elizabeth Karnes.)[16] There was evidently a large celebration on the 4th of July. It is assumed that most of the celebrating was conducted by the Union troops, although James stated there was "...excitement in camp."

> *July 20 Sunday. I have been well. Nothing occurred of*
> *importance. Received 2 letters from Bettie Karnes and*
> *B L Symms. All was well. Nothing from home yet, might*
> *Monday.(?)*

The Bettie Karnes mentioned was no doubt a relative on James' mother's side of the family. B. L. Symms was possibly a relative on his father's side. James was anxious to hear from his wife but was still waiting for a letter.

> *Camp Douglas July 23rd. Nothing of importance.*
> *Got letter from J C Heardley all well.*

> *27th. Had toothache all night last night no better yet*
> *rumoured exchange of prisoners. Great excitement in camp*
> *& city a few nights ago occasioned by a few prisoners breaking*
> *out past the guard. Got a letter from Bettie Karnes. More men*
> *put into our barracks & c. Nice Sunday to day.*

The "great excitement" James referred to occurred the night of July 23. A group of prisoners made a well-planned escape attempt. The main thrust of the escape included the use of three scaling ladders which had been constructed of boards and cleats. A tunnel was found under the stockade fence at another location. The 67th Illinois Infantry was called out at the double-quick and arrived just in time to thwart a general and widespread escape. About thirty prisoners, however, did make good their escape. The alarm bells were set off in downtown Chicago and the cavalry was soon sent galloping through the streets looking for the escapees. Col. Tucker reported that only 21 prisoners escaped.[17] Ten of the escaped prisoners were recaptured and returned to Camp Douglas four days later. More guards in a tighter line were placed around the prison barracks to deter other escape attempts.

On August 1, 1862, one of the few surviving rolls of the prisoners of war at Camp Douglas was taken. Col. Tucker had been ordered by his superiors to prepare complete and up-to-date rolls. Several additional clerks had to be hired to complete the lists. James C. Peters appears on that list as a private in the "Virginia Artillery." He was shown as having been captured at Ft. Donelson on Feb. 16.[18]

> *Camp Douglas August 5th 1862*
> *Heavy storm last night exchange still in agitation got letters*
> *from Bettie Symms & Bettie Karnes. In good hopes of being*
> *released soon. A good deal of sickness in camp one man died*
> *in our barracks two of our men sent to hospital. Nothing*
> *important.*

By this time, rumors of exchange were hot among both prisoners and their guards. Prisoner exchanges between North and South had been reinstituted in June or July. The sickness that was strong in camp during July and August was scurvy. Scurvy was

Some of the Confederate prisoners captured at Fort Donelson, TN, shortly after their arrival at Camp Douglas prison camp. They are wearing prisoner-of-war identification tags.

described as being due to confinement, "innutritious food" and hard labor, but especially to the lack of fresh vegetables. During June and July, 283 Confederate prisoners died, with 1,147 becoming ill.[19] It is possible that one of the men James referred to as being sick and sent to the hospital was Sgt. Samuel Ross of French's Battery.

> *August 16th. Have been well. No news from home yet.*
> *Nothing from father. Exchange still in agitation. Had tooth*
> *pulled. Dreams of home & wife last night. Hope to be released*
> *soon.*

Even though James had received letters from friends and other family members, he was obviously anxious for news of his wife and new baby as well as his father. Also there was still frequent talk of the possibility of exchange as James dreamed of home. He finally had the troublesome tooth pulled that had bothered him for the last four months. On August 20, 1862, Sgt. Samuel Ross of French's Battery died in the camp hospital.

> *Camp Douglas August 24*
> *Have been unwell. Feel better now. Received 5 letters last week.*
> *Exchange still in agitation. No news from home yet. Still in hopes*
> *of being released soon.*

Once again, James mentioned he received five letters in one week. The important one from his wife was evidently not among them. The diary revealed that James had constant hope of being released even though the "exchange [was] still in agitation."

On the last few pages of the diary (not in sequence with the dated narrative) are pages that are James Peters' accounting of money. The only dated entry was the one for August 26, 1862. The entries are shown together here because all the men on these pages enlisted with James at the Alvis Farm on July 27, 1861 and all were captured at Fort Donelson and incarcerated at Camp Douglas. Probably all the entries were made while at Camp Douglas.

> *Camp Douglas August 26th*
> *Dr to the following persons*
> *To Samuel Johnston   .34*
> *   -   .10   [These names had been*
> *   -   .50   erased]*
> *   -   .50*

> [Another page in the diary]
>
> | | $ | cts |
> |----------------------|---|-----|
> | *John W. Brown* | *1* | *25* |
> | *William F. Steele* | | *25* |
> | *Franklin M. Thomas* | | *30* |

The John W. Brown mentioned on this list was John Wesley Brown, the 2nd Corporal of French's Battery.

[Another page in the diary]

D To John Sarver	.15
D To Joseph Fisher	.10
D To Theodore Smith	.25
D To Winton Blankenship	.10
D To Samuel Johnston	.35
D To Roland Tracy	.50
D To D B Johnston and	.50
James Thomas	1.00
D To Frank J. Miller	.25

The Winton Blankenship mentioned on this list was Winston Blankenship, a private in French's Battery. Theodore Smith was the 4th Corporal of French's Battery and later 2nd Lieutenant of the 30th Battalion Sharpshooters after the reorganization. The D B Johnston was Daniel B. Johnson, the orderly sergeant of French's Battery at the time of their capture.

[Another page in the diary]

John Sarver	.35	
Robert Turner	.10	
James A. Thornton	.23	*[All these entries had*
T P Thornton Dr	.55	*been marked through]*
Joseph Fisher Dr	.40	
Augustus Cole Dr	.10	

The T P Thornton mentioned on this list was Thomas P. Thornton, a private in French's Battery. He died of a brain inflammation at Camp Douglas on Sept. 13, 1862 and is buried in Oakwood Cemetery in Chicago.

Suddenly things began to happen at Camp Douglas that made the prisoners ecstatic. On August 28, Col. Tucker received orders that prisoners were to be exchanged and he was to begin transferring prisoners as soon as practical.[20] This order came more than one month after the cartel to exchange all prisoners of war had been arranged by Gen. John Dix for the United States and Gen. D. H. Hill of the Confederacy.[21] The prisoners were to leave by regiments in groups of 1,000 and be transported through Cairo, Illinois and on to the exchange point at Vicksburg, Mississippi.

Sept 6. Wet rainy day. Orders to leave Douglas shortly
for to be exchanged. I am much rejoiced & in good hopes of seeing
my wife & children soon. I have been unwell for the last
three or four days. The God that has protected me will protect
my wife & children. Thanks to God.

So at last James' hopes and prayers were being answered! The formal orders to the prisoners came down to pack what few things they wanted to take with them and to be ready to march out of Camp Douglas. Even though James had been sick again, his only thoughts were of going home and seeing his wife and children. He prayed that God would protect him and his wife and children. The last three words of the entry for Sept. 6, 1862 say it all: "Thanks to God!"

As James was preparing to leave Camp Douglas, his old Confederate unit was once again being reorganized. On Sept. 1, by order of Gen. William W. Loring, French's Battery was changed from a light artillery unit to the 30th Battalion Virginia Sharpshooters.[22] This type of conversion happened when artillery companies lost their cannon or had their ranks decimated. For a time the new unit would be known as Clarke's Battalion after its commander Lt. Col. John Lyle Clarke. James' company would become Company B or Capt. Napoleon B. French's Co. At the time of the reorganization there were only about forty members of the old artillery unit in the field and forty-four others were still in Union prisons.[23] Even though unknown to James, he had just been made a sharpshooter!

Chapter VII
The Long Trip Home

At *3:00 pm, on* Saturday, September 6, 1862, James and his fellow prisoners marched out of the Camp Douglas prison for the last time. They must have felt relief, joy, and happiness when they passed through the gates. From the compound they marched to the railroad station. There they boarded the train cars for the start of their long trip south to freedom. On the official POW records of Camp Douglas, James Conrad Peters is shown as being transferred to Vicksburg for exchange.[1]

> *Camp Sept 8th on boat Dacotah*
> *Left Camp Douglas Saturday the 6th traveled by cars to Cairo 365*
> *miles. Left Camp D at 3 o'clock arrived at Cairo 8 o'clock at night*
> *on the 8th being on cars 30 hours was put on this boat last night at*
> *10 o'clock. I was very unwell on the trip but feel better this morning.*
> *A very hard trip on boat.*

It is very likely that on this first leg of their trip James and his compatriots traveled over the same tracks of the Illinois Central Railroad that had brought the prisoners to Chicago in February. At 8 pm on the evening of September 8, after a grueling ride of thirty hours on the rail cars, the prisoners reached Cairo, Illinois on the Mississippi River. Two hours later the men were put on one of eight boats for the trip down the river to the exchange point at Vicksburg.

> *Our fleet consists of the Meteor, Diligent, Dacotah, Dove, Charteau,*
> *Golden Era, Universe, Adriatic.*

Even though this entry was written in a different section of James Peters' diary it has been verified as the list of the eight boats that took James and his compatriots downriver to Vicksburg. These boats were either already in U.S. service or were commandeered for transporting the prisoners downriver for exchange.

POW Flotilla: Cairo to Vicksburg
Specifications of the Ships[2]

Adriatic: Sternwheel packet boat with wood hull, built at Shousetown, PA in 1854. Dimensions: 200 x 45 x 6.5 (feet). Weight: 424 tons. Powered by two sternwheels, each with its own set of two engines. Sank on the Missouri River Mar. 28, 1865. Raised and dismantled; hull used as a freight barge. Largest boat in the flotilla.

Charteau: No records. James possibly misspelled the name. Could have been the packet boat *Chautauque*, built in 1839 in New York, Weight: 161 tons, or more likely the *Charter*, a wood hull packet boat built at Paducah, KY in 1856.

Dacotah: Sternwheel packet boat, wood hull, built at Belle Vernon, Pennsylvania in 1858. Correct name probably *Decotah*. Weight: 230 tons. Had 13-foot draft, originally fitted with two Dahlgreen guns, one of which was probably used on the ironclad *USS Monitor*. Was at Florence, Alabama in 1861 with other ships which were asked to leave because they were built in the North. Confederates raided and burned her at Paducah, Kentucky on Mar. 25, 1864.

Diligent: Sternwheel packet boat, wood hull, built at Louisville, Kentucky in 1859. Weight: 140 tons. Smallest boat in the POW convoy. Used as U.S. troop transport and to carry sick and wounded during the war. Snagged and sank at Helena, Arkansas, Jan. 10, 1865.

Dove: Sternwheel packet boat, wood hull, built at Louisville, Kentucky in 1856. Dimensions: 147.6 x 29.3 x 5 (feet). Weight: 176 tons. Snagged and sank on the Pearl River, Mississippi, 1866.

Golden Era: Side-wheel packet boat, wood hull, built at Wheeling, Virginia (now West Virginia) in 1852. Dimensions: 178 x 29 x 5.1 (feet). Weight: 249 or 275 tons. Utilized

The side-wheel packet boat *Golden Era*, at the wharf in Cairo, Ill., in 1864. This was one of the seven ships that brought James Peters and his fellow prisoners of war to Vicksburg in September, 1862. Note the Union gunboat anchored out in the Mississippi River at upper right. Courtesy Chicago Historical Society

as troop transport by the U.S. during the war, making at least three trips to Vicksburg. Sold to a New Orleans Company in 1866. Dismantled in 1868.

Meteor: Side-wheel packet boat, wood hull, built at Louisville, Kentucky in 1857. Dimensions: 233 x 36 x 6 (feet). Weight: 417 tons. First home port was St. Louis, Missouri. Sailed the Mississippi River and transferred to U.S. War Dept. in 1864. Reported lost in the wharf fire at New Orleans on May 28, 1864. There were at least four ships with this name in service during the Civil War period.

Universe: Side-wheel packet boat, wood hull, built at Cincinnati, Ohio in 1857. Dimensions: 180 x 35 x 7 (feet). Weight: 399 tons. Three boilers. First home port was Cincinnati. Served as a transport for the U.S. on the Tennessee and Mississippi Rivers during the war. Snagged and sank on the Mississippi, Oct. 30, 1864 with loss of seventeen lives.

(Note that only two of the eight ships survived the Civil War.)

On board Dacatur* Sept 8th.

Left Cairo at 3 o'clock Sept 8 in co. with 7 other boats loaded with
prisoners & one gunboat for officers. Columbus late in evening &
about 10 o'clock at night --- I stayed all night. Feel tolerably well---.

(*James frequently interchanged the spellings of his boat. Its correct name was the Decotah.)

The Columbus mentioned by James was Columbus, Kentucky located across the Mississippi from Belmont, Missouri. Columbus, situated on a high bluff, had been the site of a large Confederate fort erected in 1861 that had housed 140 cannon. It had been called by military officers on both sides "The Gibralter of the West."[3] After the fall of Forts Henry and Donelson in February, 1862, Columbus became the next important target for Union forces. The Confederate government, having learned a hard lesson from Henry and Donelson, ordered its evacuation. By early March the fort and 138 of its cannon had been evacuated by the Confederates and it was soon occupied by Federal troops.

On board Dacotah at Memphis Tennessee Sept. 10.
Raised anchor at sunrise Sept 9 & started for Memphis passed Island
No. 10 & Ft. Pillow & anchored about 10 o'clock at night. I feel tolerable
well all day til night. I felt unwell in later part of night feel better now.
Had a pleasant dream about wife & children & house. Raised anchor
this morning about 7 o'clock & ran down to Memphis where we are now
anchored. Memphis is a very nice city expect to stay here awhile. But do
not know how long. Sept 10th at 10 o'clock

Island No. 10 was downriver from Columbus, Kentucky. It was located at a horseshoe bend in the river at the junction of Missouri, Kentucky and Tennessee, near the town of New Madrid, Missouri. It received its name by being the tenth island in the Mississippi south of its junction with the Ohio River. Ft. Pillow was another sixty or seventy miles downriver from Island No. 10 on the Tennessee side of the river, and north of Memphis. These had been two of the five forts built by the Confederates to protect the western border of the Confederacy. Island No. 10 had a history shockingly similar to Forts Henry and Donelson. After the Confederate post at New Madrid had been attacked by Union forces in March of 1862, the troops had been evacuated and moved to Island No. 10. The island was attacked by Union Flag Officer Andrew Foote's gunboats, which forced the Island garrison to surrender on April 7.[4] Seven thousand Confederates were hemmed in by Union troops in the swamps and surrendered that day. On June 4 and 5, Fort Pillow was abandoned by the Confederates. These two river forts fell while James Peters was a prisoner of war at Camp Douglas. As his boat passed these two sites, James must have felt a kinship to the men who had occupied these two fallen Confederate forts and probably thought again of his own capture at Fort Donelson.

Once again, James had pleasant dreams of home and family. He had experienced a touch of sickness aboard the boat, as had many of his fellow passengers. When the flotilla anchored near Memphis, he was feeling much better. Memphis was the home of almost 30,000 people and was of double importance due to its strategic position on the Mississippi River.[5] When Nashville had been evacuated earlier in 1862, the state legislature had moved to Memphis. Governor Isham Harris proclaimed Memphis to be the new state capital. By the end of March, however, the legislature had adjourned and state officials had fled. After the defeat of the Confederate flotilla on the Mississippi the town was occupied by Federal troops. All of west Tennessee was in Union hands by the time James and his fellow prisoners anchored at Memphis.

> On board Dacotah at Helena Arkansas Sept 12 at 7 o'clock.
> Left Memphis Sept 11 at 3 o'clock & passed down the river to this place. Arrived here last night & this morning lying at anchor above the city. Nothing unusual occurred on the voyage, feel tolerable this morning. Very nice country along the river.
>
> Sept. 13th.
> Lay at anchor all day yesterday & today until about 4 'clock when we raised anchor & ran until about 10 o'clock at night when we anchored for the night. Large army encamped along the river below Helena.

After having stayed the better part of two days at Memphis, James and the other prisoners continued their voyage downriver. On Sept. 13, two of James Peters' fellow soldiers from French's Battery died.[6] Both had enlisted with James at the Alvis Farm back in Mercer County, Virginia. One was Pvt. Thomas P. Thornton. Thornton had been ill with a brain inflammation and had been left behind when the other prisoners were released. He died in the Camp Douglas prison hospital. The other soldier was Pvt. Benjamin Pendleton. He died aboard one of the boats while anchored near Helena. We do not know if he died on board the *Dacotah*, or aboard one of the other boats of the flotilla.

The "large army" that could be seen encamped south of Helena was probably part of Union Gen. Grant's forces that had been dispersed along the Mississippi from Columbus south to Memphis.

> On board Dacotah Sept 14th 1862
>   Mississippi
> Raised anchor at daylight this morning & ran very steadily all day until about 8 o'clock at night when we anchored. Passed Napoleon a considerable town on the Arkansas shore and several other small towns. Nothing of importance occurred. I feel better this morning than I have for some days past. I am in good hopes of soon getting off this old boat where I can get something to eat.

Napoleon was another river town some sixty miles downriver from Helena, located on the Arkansas shore of the Mississippi. After living on board the boat for six days, it is understandable that James wanted to get "...off this old boat where I can get something to eat." The food supplied to the prisoners was barely enough to sustain life.

Route of James Conrad Peters from Camp Douglas,
Chicago, Ill., to his home in Mercer Co., WV.
Sept-Oct, 1862

On board Dacotah Sept 15th 1862
       Mississippi
Raised anchor about 10 o'clock & ran down to just above Vicksburg &
anchored. Feel tolerable well this day and in high hopes of getting of[f]
today.

Sept 16th. Lay at anchor all day today. A boat came up from Vicksburg
& took our officers down. Bad rainy day disagreeable Felt tolerable well
today wrote two letters. Been in hopes getting off all day but did not.

At last the great day was near. With the exchange at Vicksburg for Union prisoners of war now eminent, the men were certainly anxious to get off the boats and head for home. At this point the men may not have known if they would actually get a leave to visit their families and homes, or if they would be immediately returned to duty with their units. On Sept 16, a boat came up from Vicksburg and took all the officers down for exchange. The Confederate officers were needed to work out the organization and disposition of the other Confederate soldiers such as James Peters.

On boat Dacotah Sept 17th 1862
Lay at anchor all day. Prisoners off 4 boats released, nice day, feel
tolerable well.
Nothing important occurred.

So as each boat of prisoners was processed, one boat at a time, James had to wait for his turn to come. His boat of prisoners had now waited at anchor for two days.

Vicksburg, Mississippi Sept 18th.
We were released today at about 2 o'clock after having been prisoners
7 months & 2 days. We were marched to Vicksburg & are now quartered
in church. Thanks be to him who has preserved me through hardships
& danger & many temptations.

From Camp D to Cairo	*365 miles*
from Cairo to Vicksburg	*700*
	1065 miles

After leaving our quarters for the night I took a walk over the beautiful
& once populous city of Vicksburg but which now looks desolute &
deserted. The ravages of shot & shell are to be seen in every quarter.
The beautiful church in which we are now staying has been torn with
shell. O the horror of war they are to be seen in this place. May God put
a speedy end to this unholy war is my prayer.

James, once again recording dates and mileage as he had in his travels before the War, noted the distance he traveled, and more importantly, the total length of time he had been a prisoner of war. After his formal exchange and return to the Confederates, he was given lodging and had time to walk through Vicksburg. In his longest diary entry of the War, James then wrote about what he observed while touring the war-torn city. His observations of the "ravages of shot and shell" were certainly understandable, based on the city's ordeal over the few months prior to his arrival. It was estimated that between 20,000 and 25,000 shells had been hurled into the city by Union guns.[7] But Vicksburg had survived the siege, frustrating the efforts of the Union fleet and a 3,000 man land force under Brig. Gen. Thomas Williams. The Union forces had withdrawn. They would return, however, in 1863, and Vicksburg would fall in July. Also in this entry James thanked God for seeing him through his hardships and asked Him to "...put a speedy end to this unholy war..." The damage to private homes, churches and buildings of the "beautiful & once populous city" must certainly have been a depressing sight to James and his friends. The church that became James' home while in Vicksburg was probably the Methodist or Baptist. Both were damaged by shelling during this period. The Catholic church was also downtown, but may not have sustained any damage until the siege of 1863.

> *Vicksburg Mississippi Sept 19th.*
> *Stayed this day in the city & strolled about over the city, took a good*
> *wash & put on clean clothes. Got some beautiful flowers.*
>
> *Sept 20th. Spent this day strolling about over Vicksburg. Got dinner*
> *& supper at a gentleman's house. Feel tolerable well.*
>
> *Sept 21st. Got orders to be at depot at 6 o'clock to go to Jackson.*
> *Went to Depot but did not get off & came back to church and strolled*
> *about city got supper at house &c &c &c.*

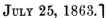

JULY 25, 1863.]

View of the city of Vicksburg before the War. The old courthouse is in the upper left background of the picture. *Harper's Weekly*

After the shock of the first day's walking tour of war-ravaged Vicksburg, the next three days were spent in seeing more of the town and engaging in the normal activities that had been so rare at Camp Douglas. Among these were taking "a good wash" and putting on clean clothes. For James Peters this also included locating some beautiful flowers. Even in the midst of a war beauty could still be recognized and appreciated. James then found some kind people to eat his meals with. On the fourth day the men received orders to report to the train station to board the train to Jackson, Mississippi. But once again, transportation was delayed and James went back to his quarters at the war-ravaged church.

> *Jackson Mississippi Sept 22.*
> *Left Vicksburg at 2 o'clock & after a very pleasant ride on the cars*
> *landed at this place, 4 1/2 miles, at 5 o'clock and was marched*
> *through the city & about 1 mile outside & lay down in the open field*
> *for the night.*

James Peters boarded the cars of the Vicksburg & Jackson Railroad for the short ride to the capital city of Mississippi. Jackson had been the site of the Mississippi secession convention and in 1860 had a population of about 3,798 souls. Jackson was also a Confederate command center for logistics for both Confederate and state troops. Upon arriving there, the ex-POWs marched through the town to an open field where they slept that night.

> *Sept 26th. We are encamped in the old fair ground.*
> *Nothing of importance occurred. Fair warm weather.*
> *Wrote letter home yesterday. Got orders this evening to*
> *prepare to leave this place in the morning at 7 o'clock.*

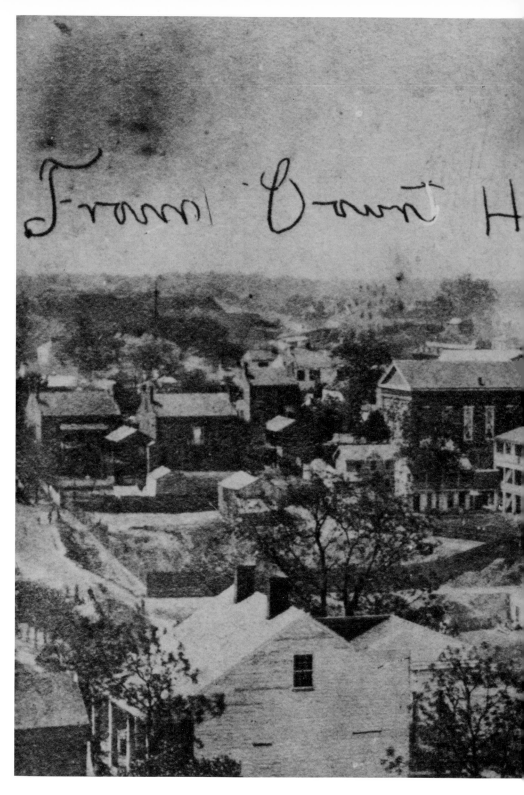

Downtown Vicksburg, MS circa 1860 or 1861. Writing on original photo says "From Court House Dome, V'burg, Miss." The church in the upper middle of photo is the Baptist Church and could have been where James and his compatriots were housed for a week after their exchange. Courtesy Old Court House Museum and Davis Memorial, Vicksburg, MS

Artillery position at reconstructed Confederate fortifications, Vicksburg National Military Park. Fortifications overlook the Mississippi River in the background.

James and his compatriots rested for four days and finally received orders to be ready to leave on Friday.

> *Meridian Mississippi Sept 27.*
> *Got up this morning at daylight & left Jackson at 11 1/2 o'clock*
> *& landed at this place at 12 o'clock at night. Wet rainy weather.*

At daylight on Saturday, Sept 27, 1862, James and his friends boarded the Southern Railroad train for the ride to Meridian. Meridian was a rail junction, as the Southern and the Mobile & Ohio Railroads crossed there. It was also a supply depot for the Confederate troops in that area. After serving briefly as the state capital it would be burned to the ground only two years later by attacking Union forces.

> *Sept 28th. Mobile Ala.*
> *Slept in cars, eat breakfast at R R house paid $1.00.*
> *Left Meridian at 9 o'clock and arrived at Mobile at 9 o'clock*
> *at night. Poor country, piny, wet & sandy.*

After arriving in Meridian, the men had nowhere else to sleep other than the railroad cars. James was able to go up into town the next morning and buy breakfast at the railroad boarding house for the inflated fee of a dollar. At Meridian, James boarded the cars of the Mobile & Ohio Railroad, which ran south to Mobile, Alabama. James remarked that the country he saw along the tracks through southern Mississippi was "poor country, piny, wet & sandy."

Mobile was the state of Alabama's only seaport and was the largest city in the state, boasting a population of between 30,000 and 35,000 inhabitants. Mobile was located at the mouth of the Tensaw River and had access to the Gulf of Mexico. At the start of the war it was second only to New Orleans in the exporting of cotton. The city was known as the "Paris of the Confederacy."[8] In 1860 it ranked as the seventh in population of major southern cities. It was a crucial port for the blockaded Confederacy and was also the site of training camps for Confederate soldiers in the area.

> *Pollard, Ala. Sept 29th*
> *Left Mobile at 12 o'clock & crossed M[obile] bay on boat, 22 miles.*
> *Took cars at 3 & arrived at this place at dark. 50 Miles.*

After staying only one night in Mobile, the men boarded a steamboat and steamed the 22 miles across Mobile Bay. On the eastern side of the bay, the men boarded the cars of the Alabama & Florida Railroad at the little town of Tensas Station. (This stretch of rails may have been known at the time as the Great Northern Railroad.)

> *Montgomery, Ala Sept 30th*
> *Slept upon the cars. Left P[ollard] at 5 o'clock & arrived*
> *at this place at 4 o'clock distance 112 miles. Camped for the night.*

After once again having to sleep in the railroad cars, they left the little Alabama town of Pollard and headed northeast. They stopped next at the Alabama state capital, where they camped. (At least they avoided sleeping in the cars, again.)

Montgomery also must have been an exciting town. It was Alabama's second largest city in 1860, with a population of about 9,000. In February of 1861 the Confederate States had been organized at Montgomery, and Jefferson Davis was inaugurated as its president there. In May of 1861 the Confederate capital had been moved to Richmond. Montgomery was an important rail center as connecting railroads of different gauges intersected there. There were seven military hospitals in the city and small arms for the Confederacy were being manufactured in the town. It was also a major supply depot for the troops in the area.

> *Atlanta, Ga. Oct 1st 1862*
> *Strolled through town & washed & put on clean clothes.*
> *Left M at 4 o'clock & arrived at West Point at 10 o'clock &*
> *changed cars & left for this place. Arrived here at daylight*
> *October 2nd Ran all night slept in car a little feel tolerable*
> *well this day.*

James was able to see some of the town of Montgomery and get clean clothes, before boarding the train for the next leg of his journey. At Montgomery the men boarded the cars of the Montgomery & West Point Railroad. The tracks in that area became 4' - 8 1/2" gauge track, different from the 5' gauge track in the rest of that part of the South.[9] At West Point, near the Alabama-Georgia state line, the tracks probably went back to 5' gauge, and required a complete change to another train. At that junction the railroad became known as the Montgomery & Atlanta Railroad.

On October 2nd, James arrived at the largest rail center south of Richmond—the city of Atlanta. In 1860 Atlanta had a population of almost 10,000 people. It was not only a busy rail center, but iron and steel rolling mills and machine shops were located there. Major repairs for steam engines and railroad cars were also performed at some of these shops. This was also the location of the Confederate Quartermaster Department headquarters and therefore a major supply station.

> *Dalton Georgia Oct 2.*
> *Left Atlanta at 9 o'clock & arrived at this place at dark.*

After only a one night stay in Atlanta, the men boarded the cars of the Western & Atlantic Railroad to continue their journey north. At Dalton, the railroad forked with the Western & Atlantic turning northwest to Chattanooga, only about thirty miles away. James and his traveling companions changed to the other fork, on the East Tennessee & Georgia Railroad which headed northeast.

> *Knoxville Tenn Oct 3.*
> *Left Dalton at 3 1/2 o'clock & arrived here at 4 o'clock at night.*
> *Felt very unwell today. Headache very bad.*

Even though James was sick, he probably realized he was retracing his steps of the last week of December of 1861 as his train rolled into Knoxville. He and the men of French's Battery had passed through Knoxville on their way to Ft. Donelson. He would also come to Knoxville one more time before this terrible war would end.

> *Bristol, Tenn Oct 4th midnight.*
> *Left Knoxville at 11 o'clock & arrived here at 11 o'clock at night.*
> *Came on passenger train.*

The men left Knoxville on the East Tennessee & Virginia Railroad. (This railroad was also called the Virginia & East Tennessee.) Once again James and his compatriots rolled into Bristol. They had slept there the night of Dec. 28, 1861 on their trip to Ft. Donelson. Here two rail lines met, but freight and passengers had to be hauled by wagon between the stations. At least James had a real seat on a passenger train, instead of riding on the floor of the freight cars.

> *Lynchburg, Virginia Oct 5*
> *Left Bristol at 12 o'clock last night & arrived here at 6 o'clock*
> *took quarters in tobacco factory.*

The men left Bristol and rolled through Dublin Depot, Virginia, where French's Battery had received their cannon during Christmas week of 1861. How different the circumstances had been between James' two trips through Dublin! At Lynchburg the men found quarters in the old tobacco factory building.

Lynchburg was another principal supply depot for the Virginia Confederates. The Confederate War Dept. had stockpiled clothing, munitions, and food there. The town was of double importance because it was considered far behind the front lines of the fighting. The railroads connected here, with the 5' gauge tracks continuing east to Petersburg. James and his train went onto more 4' - 8 1/2" gauge tracks that turned north to Charlottesville.

Richmond,Virginia Oct 6th.
Left Lynchburg at 6 o'clock & arrived here at 6 1/2 o'clock.
Went via Charlottsville & Gordonsville & Beaver Dam Station.

At Charlottsville the Virginia & Tennessee Railroad met the Virginia Central Railroad. Charlottsville was also a large hospital center for the Confederate Army in Virginia. James may have been able to see Monticello, the home of Thomas Jefferson from the tracks of the Virginia Central. At Gordonsville, the railroad forked again, with the Orange & Alexandria Railroad continuing north to Alexandria, while James stayed on the Virginia Central, which turned southeast toward Richmond. About twelve miles past Beaver Dam Station on the North Anna River, the railroad forked at Hanover Junction. Both the Richmond, Fredericksburg & Potomac and the Virginia Central Railroads headed south into Richmond.

At 6:30 pm on Monday, Oct. 6th, 1862, James Conrad Peters arrived at the busy and bustling capital of the Confederate States of America. In 1860 Richmond was already a large city with a population of over 37,000. The city grew tremendously after the Confederate capital was moved there in May of 1861. Richmond was the home of the largest flour mill in the world, the Gallego, which had shipped to Australia and South America before the war.[10] It had also been the home of the largest tobacco market in the world, supporting sixty factories. More important to the Confederacy was the Tredegar Iron Works, the second largest foundry in the United States before the war. After the start of the war Tredegar produced cannon and iron plate and served as a model for southern industrialization. New blast furnaces had been opened only a few months before James' arrival. Richmond was also a transportation center, with five railroads intersecting there: The Richmond & York River ran east to West Point, the Richmond, Fredericksburg, & Potomac (RF&P) ran north, the Virginia Central which had brought James into town came from Charlottesville by way of Gordonsville, the Richmond & Petersburg connected to Weldon, and the Richmond & Danville was the city's main link south. The James River and Kanawha Canal also ran west to Lynchburg. Richmond was of course the social center of Virginia and the Confederacy. Receptions and dances were held frequently and the business of the Confederate Government prompted many meetings, balls, and get-togethers. A major arsenal and armory were also located there, along with Libby Prison, Castle Thunder and other smaller prisons. Two of the largest hospitals were located there: Camp Winder and Chimborazo. Since over 7,000 men from the area served in the Confederate Army, large training camps were set up in or near the town. Camp Lee was the largest and most well known. It was located on West Broad Street at the fairgrounds. Camp Lee was the central site for military court proceedings in Richmond and many court-martials and executions took place there.

View of Richmond, Va., 1865. Frank Leslie's *Illustrated* Newspaper

Oct 7th.
Stayed at Depot until 10 o'clock when we were marched through
Richmond to Camp Lee & put up tents & drew cooking vessels &
went into camp.

Oct 8th. Stayed about our tents all day today. Cooking, eating &c.
I have felt very unwell today got very bad cold & cough & bowel
complaint.

For the first time since being exchanged at Vicksburg on September 18, James and his fellow ex-POWs were able to get some rest in a semi-permanent location. Unfortunately James was ill again with the flu. It appears he only traded the unpleasantness of traveling and sleeping in freight cars for the ills of camp life. At least now James could cook some cornbread and have some real coffee; rationed of course.

Dublin Depot Oct 13th.
Left Richmond the 11th at 6 o'clock & landed at this place
at 1 o'clock yesterday a distance 250 miles. We lay under the
woodshed last night. Very damp drizzly weather.
Very bad cold yet.

After only staying a week in Richmond, James was on the move again. But this was the last leg home. James backtracked his train route that had brought him into Richmond. He passed again through Charlottesville, Lynchburg, and stopped at Dublin Depot in Pulaski County. James still had a bad cold, which was not helped by having to sleep under a woodshed on the night he arrived at Dublin.

Oct 14. Left Dublin this morning at daylight & traveled to
Gilestown. Got there at dark put up at the tavern for night.

As there were no railroads from Dublin Depot north during the Civil War, James either walked or found a horse for the remainder of his trip home. He probably walked, as he noted it took him all day until dark to travel the distance of only about twenty miles to what is now Pearisburg, the county seat of Giles County. He was able to obtain a roof over his head at the local tavern, unlike the previous night.

Oct 15th. Left Gilestown this morning at 8 o'clock got home at
3 o'clock after having been absent 10 months & 2 days.

James rode or walked the remaining distance to his home in Mercer County. In keeping with his attention to details, he noted he had been gone from home exactly ten months and two days. How wonderful the reunion with his family must have been! Of course he was overjoyed to be in the arms of his wife, Polly Ann, again. His oldest daughter, Mary Elizabeth had just celebrated her second birthday a month before his homecoming. His second daughter, Sarah Emeline, who had been born while he was a prisoner of war at Camp Douglas, would now meet her father. She was only four months old when her father held her for the first time.

James had certainly seen a large part of both the United States and the Confederate States since leaving Camp Douglas almost five weeks before. He had traveled through or touched ten states over the hundreds of miles between the two locations. To reach home he had ridden on ten different railroads, had also traveled by steamboat and on foot. But at last he was home, somewhere he had longed to be many times over the last "10 months & 2 days."

Even though James had yet to report to his new unit, the 30th Battalion Virginia Sharpshooters, his promotion to 1st corporal was effective November 1, 1862.[11]

Chapter VIII

Back to War

2nd campaign Narrows New River Nov 11.
Left home yesterday at 10 'clock & traveled on foot to this place
arrived here at 3 o'clock & went into camp. Very tired & feet
very sore.

After resting at home for almost four weeks, James left on foot Monday, Nov. 10, 1862, to report to his unit. He walked the few miles to Peterstown in Monroe County, and then the remaining seven miles to Narrows in Giles Co., Virginia. It is understandable that James' feet were very sore and he was tired upon reaching the camp of the 30th Battalion Sharpshooters.

The Narrows of New River was an important crossing during the Civil War, as it was one of the few places where the river could be forded by troops. On several occasions during the War when "regular" troops were not watching the Narrows, the Virginia Reserve forces were called out to picket the crossing. Now for the first time since his capture at Fort Donelson in February, James would meet up with what few soldiers were left of his original artillery company. His old company was now designated Company B of the 30th Battalion. It was still commanded by Capt. Napoleon B. French. The unit had been organized as a sharpshooters battalion on September 1. The battalion consisted of six companies, lettered "A" through "F." Company A was formerly known as Capt. Stephen Adams' Company, Virginia Light Artillery, which had also been captured at Ft. Donelson.[1] Through September and into October James' company had been stationed at Princeton, in Mercer County, now West Virginia.

19th. Still in the same camp. Very cloudy damp weather.
Health tolerable good. Have received letter from home and --- Wrote
home Sunday. No news of ----- in camp on the river one mile
above the mouth of Wolfe.

The normal drudgeries of camp life set in. James received a letter from home and wrote an answering letter during the week. He noted they were on the river one mile above the mouth of Wolfe. Wolfe Creek in Giles County flows east and empties into the New River near the Narrows crossing. This location is now the town of Narrows. Also on the 19th of November Napoleon B. French resigned as captain of Company B due to his age (51 years). He had also just been appointed superintendent of roads in his home county.

Camp Narrows Nov 26th 1862.
Still at our old camp Nothing of importance has occurred lately.
Got a letter from home all well. I have had my health very well.

30th. Nothing of importance. Still in old camp. A man of
importance---was here. My health very tolerable. Cool night & ---

With the month of November coming to an end, James noted that nothing of importance had occurred. Someone important visited the camp around November 30. James
mentioned the nights were getting cool.

> *Dec 6th. Cold rainy weather. ----I am in very good health yet I*
> *know not of patience still it is promised I must -- -------.*

As winter approached in the New River Valley, James continued in good health, but
evidently was becoming impatient. The boredom of nearly a month of camp life was
taking its toll. James was probably also wondering if he would spend another Christmas away from his family and perhaps he was trying to obtain a leave to visit them.

> *Fbry 3d 1863*
> *In winter quarters near Pearisburg. Nothing has occurred out*
> *of the ordinary routine of camp life. Have been well. Some stormy*
> *weather & cold. Have been at home thrice --- Sundays. I have*
> *------------ hard times. No news of Yankees coming up yet hope there*
> *will be fight soon.*

In early December the battalion's camp was moved to more permanent winter
quarters near the county seat of Pearisburg. Since the camp was located near James'
home, he was able to visit there on three Sundays. This of course helped break the
boredom of winter quarters. The camp was named Camp Clarke in honor of his unit's
commander, Col. James Lyle Clarke.

Here abruptly the dated diary entries of James Conrad Peters end. The diary was
probably left at home on a leave of absence. It is also possible that James started a
second volume which has not been found.

Much of the following account of the 30th Battalion Sharpshooters is taken from
the diary of another member of the unit, Sgt. Major John M. Schowen.[2] Even though
Schowen was born in Monroe County, Virginia, at the age of fifteen he moved with his
family to a farm near Spencer in Roane County. There he became a neighbor and
acquaintance of Samuel Sinnett whose plantation Christian Snidow Peters, James
Conrad Peters' father, had managed before the war.

The 30th Battalion Sharpshooters remained in camp near Narrows, Virginia until
April 19, 1863. On that date the men were ordered with the other units of their brigade
to move to Saltville in Washington County. Sometime during this period or in the next
month the 30th Battalion Sharpshooters was assigned to Wharton's Brigade. The brigade was commanded by Col. Gabriel C. Wharton, who had been the commanding
officer of the 51st Virginia Infantry Regiment. Wharton and the 51st Virginia had also
fought at Ft. Donelson, but had escaped capture with Gen. John Floyd on the riverboats.
Col. Wharton would not receive his commission as a brigadier general until later in
the summer. Other units composing the brigade were the 51st Virginia, the 50th Virginia, and Stamp's Battery of artillery.

Before the unit left camp several men deserted. They had received the news that
they were being ordered further east into Virginia, and knew this would be their last
chanch to see their families. (The majority of the men who deserted from the various

companies were from Mercer and Monroe Counties which adjoined Giles County, the location of Camp Clarke.) Some of these men deserted while on the march to Saltville. James Conrad Peters does not appear on any of the official rosters as having been one of the deserters.

30th Battalion Virginia Sharpshooters, CSA
Deserted From Camp Clarke, Narrows, Virginia
April, 1863

Companies:	Apr. 18	Apr. 19	Apr. 20	Totals:	Returned*
A		4	1	5	3
B	8	5		13	3
C		7		7	1
D		8	2	10	2
E				0	
F				0	
Totals:	8	24	3	35	9

*Appears on rosters as having returned voluntarily.

The men remained near Saltville until June 10, when they were ordered back to the Narrows. After a few days in camp, the sharpshooters were ordered again into the Virginia Valley. They marched out of camp on July 9 and arrived at Staunton on the evening of the 12th, where they went into camp and remained until the 17th of July when they were ordered to Winchester.

On June 20, 1863 the state of West Virginia was formed from Virginia. The new state included the counties of Mercer and Monroe and therefore the home of James Conrad Peters. Since West Virginia was admitted to the Union as a northern state, James and his Confederate compatriots from that area were now officially from "behind enemy lines."

At this time Gen. Robert E. Lee's army was falling back from its march into Maryland. Wharton's Brigade, along with Wade Hampton's cavalry marched in the rear of the large army. They next went into camp near Fisher's Hill and remained there until the 4th of August when they marched up the valley to New Market. There they crossed the Blue Ridge Mountains and arrived at Orange C.H. (now the town of Orange) about the 10th of August. The remainder of August and most of September were occupied with marching and picketing in the Valley. The brigade was next ordered back to Saltville. The men camped near there until the 23rd of September, when they were ordered to Tennessee.

The battalion was pulled back into Virginia about the middle of October, when the Union forces were making raids near Bristol. They were engaged in a brief skirmish near there, in which they turned back a unit of Union cavalry. The men returned to Abingdon, Virginia arriving there the evening of October 15. They were exhausted from the marching and counter-marching of the last few weeks. Outside of Abingdon, the men built temporary breast works, expecting an attack. Gen. John McCausland's Brigade joined with the men of the 30th Battalion at the breastworks. The Union force, however, did not attack and instead withdrew. The Confederates were ordered to join Gen. James Longstreet's forces in Tennessee. They went as far as Blountville, Tennessee, where they went into camp until the 22nd of November. On the 24th of November the men crossed the Holston River near Kingsport. John Schowen reported that the river was four feet deep and covered in ice. The ground was also frozen solid.

When the men were within thirteen miles of Knoxville they were ordered to halt and go into camp. Gen. James Longstreet's Confederate infantry was in position to attack the Union force that had retreated to Knoxville. Other Confederate units in place containing men from southern West Virginia were the men of Gen. "Grumble" Jones' cavalry brigade and the men of the 8th Virginia Cavalry.[3] After dark on November 28, Longstreet attacked the Union forces near Fort Sanders. The Confederates poured into a wide ditch in front of the Union position, and due to a miscalculation as to the depth of the ditch, were subjected to murderous fire down into the trench. "The moat or ditch around the fort was nearly eight feet deep, with almost perpendicular walls. The dirt was all thrown on the inside, thus increasing the height of the inside walls."[4] The Confederates were stopped. The next day was occupied with the Confederates, under a flag of truce, removing the killed and wounded from the ditch. Longstreet and his army stayed in front of the defenses until the second or third of December. The Confederate Army abandoned their position and headed north. On Dec. 5, the 30th Battalion was ordered back to Bean's Station. With them were the men of the 8th Virginia Cavalry and the cavalry of "Grumble" Jones. The men traveled over the mud roads to Bean's Station, where there was a battle with Union forces, but there is no evidence that the men of the 30th Battalion were involved. They then moved back to Rogersville, Tennessee where they went into camp, remaining there until the end of December.

On New Years' Day, 1864, the men of the 30th Battalion marched to Whitesburg in Greene County, Virginia. It was extremely cold and the men suffered from frostbite. They spent the remainder of the winter near Bull's Gap, Tennessee where they picketed the roads in that vicinity. There were also Union troops in that area, as a few men of the 30th Battalion were captured while on picket duty. On the 23rd of March, the men broke camp and marched to Greenville, before heading on to Bristol. The men went into camp three miles outside of Bristol on April Fool's Day. They then moved back to Abingdon where they stayed until the 29th of April.

While encamped near Abingdon, a disturbing incident of war occurred. This incident became burned in the minds of James Conrad Peters and his compatriots. On April 15, all the men of the battalion were ordered out to stand at attention. A private in Company E of the 30th Battalion, John H. Jones, who had enlisted in Franklin County, Virginia was executed as a deserter. 1st Lt. Cephas M. Obenchain of Company D, who was from Monroe County, was in command of the firing squad. Jones had deserted three times, and when captured for the second offense, had been sentenced to fifty lashes from a cat of nine-tails. There would not be a fourth time for Private Jones.

On the 29th of April the men marched again to the rail-head at Bristol. There the

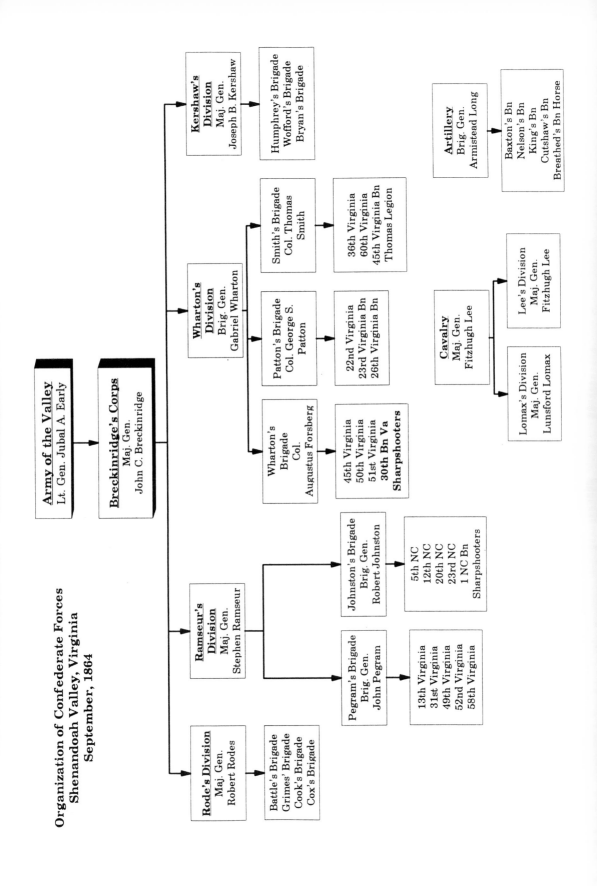

**Organization of Confederate Forces
Shenandoah Valley, Virginia
September, 1864**

Army of the Valley
Lt. Gen. Jubal A. Early

Breckinridge's Corps
Maj. Gen.
John C. Breckinridge

Kershaw's Division
Maj. Gen.
Joseph B. Kershaw

Humphrey's Brigade
Wofford's Brigade
Bryan's Brigade

Wharton's Division
Brig. Gen.
Gabriel Wharton

Smith's Brigade
Col. Thomas Smith

36th Virginia
60th Virginia
45th Virginia Bn
Thomas Legion

Patton's Brigade
Col. George S. Patton

22nd Virginia
23rd Virginia Bn
26th Virginia Bn

Wharton's Brigade
Col.
Augustus Forsberg

45th Virginia
50th Virginia
51st Virginia
30th Bn Va Sharpshooters

Ramseur's Division
Maj. Gen.
Stephen Ramseur

Johnston's Brigade
Brig. Gen.
Robert Johnston

5th NC
12th NC
20th NC
23rd NC
1 NC Bn
Sharpshooters

Pegram's Brigade
Brig. Gen.
John Pegram

13th Virginia
31st Virginia
49th Virginia
52nd Virginia
58th Virginia

Rode's Division
Maj. Gen.
Robert Rodes

Battle's Brigade
Grimes' Brigade
Cook's Brigade
Cox's Brigade

Artillery
Brig. Gen.
Armistead Long

Baxton's Bn
Nelson's Bn
King's Bn
Cutshaw's Bn
Breathed's Bn Horse

Cavalry
Maj. Gen.
Fitzhugh Lee

Lee's Division
Maj. Gen.
Fitzhugh Lee

Lomax's Division
Maj. Gen.
Lunsford Lomax

men boarded the train cars and rode to Dublin Depot in Pulaski County. They only stayed one day before moving to Giles C.H. (now Pearisburg). They remained near Pearisburg until the 4th of May. Even though very close to home, we have no way of knowing if James Peters was able to obtain leave to visit his family in the new state of West Virginia.

The men then marched east through Monroe County to Covington, where they again boarded the train. They arrived at Staunton, Virginia on the 10th of May, 1864. From that area they marched through Harrisonburg on the 14th of May and returned to the vicinity of New Market.

At New Market the forces of Wharton's Brigade, including the 30th Battalion, were joined with those of Gen. John Echols, a Monroe County native. Also called out to increase the Confederate lines was the cadet corps from the Virginia Military Institute. The cadets were technically part of the reserve forces and were activated under that regulation. Combined with this force were Gen. John Imboden's cavalry and the artillery of Chapman and Jackson's Batteries. Gen. John Breckinridge arrived on the morning of May 15th and assumed command. Breckinridge was another political general, having been the youngest man to have been elected vice-president before the war. Breckinridge organized his field forces with the 51st and 62nd Virginia Infantry of Wharton's Brigade in front, followed by the 22nd Virginia, 23rd and 26th Battalions of infantry, with the 30th Battalion covering the front and left flank as skirmishers.[5] At this early stage, the VMI cadets were held in reserve. The Union line facing them consisted of the 123rd Ohio, the 18th Connecticut, Kleiser's Battery, and the 34th Massachusetts. James Peters and the men of the 30th Battalion began skirmishing with the Union forces between 11 a.m. and noon. "The Southerners easily forced the Northern skirmish line out of New Market and realigned their ranks in preparation for an attack on the Unionists' primary position anchored north of town on Bushong's Hill."[6]

In a steady downpour, the Confederates pushed the Federal's first line back. At a fence near the Bushong House the 51st and 62nd Virginia Regiments were stopped due to the firepower of the Federal artillery. At this point a company of Missourians, unofficially attached to the 62nd Virginia as Company O were able to pick-off many of the Federal gunners. The Federals attacked but were repulsed. With much trepidation, Breckinridge ordered the VMI cadets into the front line. He was heard to state something resembling "Put the boys in, and may God forgive me for the order."[7] The Confederate line surged forward, including Wharton's Brigade and the 30th Battalion. John Schowen related: "...the Yankee battery commenced firing on us...I thought I would not live another minute, finally the line of battery was brought up and we chased the Yankees back."[8] The VMI cadets charged the Federal artillery position and captured the battery with a shout. Union Gen. Franz Sigel's forces were soon in full retreat.

Even though we know the position of the 30th Battalion Sharpshooters at the beginning of the battle, when they were deployed on the Confederate left as skirmishers, it is more difficult to pinpoint their exact location at the height of the battle:

> It is known that at least some of the men of this command were thrown
> forward as skirmishers in the first part of the battle, and it seems probable

that the different portions of the Battalion were not reunited afterward, but fought in fragments attached to other commands. Part of the Battalion skirmished before the 51st Regiment. When the battle was joined it fell back into the space between the 51st and the 62nd Regiments, the space into which the Cadets entered also. There are reasons for believing that another part of the Battalion was on the right between the 22nd and the 23d [Regiments].[9]

While all the Confederate units fought valiantly, the day in history belonged to the VMI cadets. These 247 cadets, aged from 15 to 25, commanded by Lt. Col. Scott Shipp charged through a rainstorm, took Bushong's Hill and routed the enemy. Breckinridge later rode up the hill and congratulated the cadets, and ordered them to fall out. Ten of the cadets had been killed in the charge and 47 wounded.[10] Casualties in James C. Peters' unit were numerous:

30th Battalion Virginia. Sharpshooters, CSA
Casualties: Battle of New Market, Virginia[11]
May 15, 1864
Total Engaged: 347[12]

	KIA	MWIA	WIA	MIA	Totals:
Companies:					
A		1	10	1	12
B			6	3	9
C		1	5		6
D	1	2	2	1	6
E			9	2	11
F	1	2	0		3
F & S			1		1
	======	======	======	======	======
Totals:	2	6	33	7	48

Casualties as Percent of Total Engaged: 14%

Abbreviations:
KIA – Killed in action
MWIA – Mortally wounded in action
WIA – Wounded in action
MIA – Missing in action
F & S – Field and staff officers

The importance of the Confederate victory at New Market was twofold: first, had Gen. Sigel's Union troops not been stopped, the Valley of Virginia might have been occupied before the wheat crop was harvested, and secondly the Virginia Central Railroad would have fallen into Union hands.

The Confederates were tired, wet, and hungry that night. They built up their campfires and dried their clothes. The 30th Battalion brewed some coffee that had been

Charge of the VMI cadets at the Battle of New Market, Va., May 15, 1864.

captured from the Union camp and it was a welcome libation that evening. The next morning (May 16) the men broke camp and marched toward Staunton, which they reached on May 18. The following day the men boarded railroad cars and were transported to Charlottesville. For the next week the men served picket duty around Hanover Junction and the bridge over the North River. Early on the morning of the 29th, they arrived near the vicinity of Cold Harbor and began building breastworks. Already present were Longstreet's Corps and that of Gen. A. P. Hill. Schowen stated that the enemy was already fortified in their front. This Union army facing the Confederates was the army of U. S. Grant and Phil Sheridan. The firing began on the evening of the 29th. On the evening of the next day the 30th Battalion and the remainder of Wharton's Brigade moved back about a 1/2 mile and built a new line of breastworks. June 1 dawned as a pleasant and beautiful day. Late in the day the Federals mounted a fierce attack on the Confederate line. The line broke in a few places, but before night the Confederates had succeeded in regaining their position. On June 2, the battalion moved again and erected new breastworks. On June 3, the Union forces began firing before daylight. John Schowen stated the firing lasted all day. Participants stated that the Union infantry force was arranged into lines ten columns deep. A young private in the 22nd Virginia Infantry also from West Virginia, James H. Mays, remembered the day in his memoirs:

> Against our battlements and army General Grant at once threw the weight of
> his immense force. It was a fearful and awe-inspiring sight! On comes
> the long blue line across the field, the measured tread of their marching
> punctuated by the heavy beat of their drums and by the booming of artillery,
> theirs and our own. When they came within rifle range we let them have a
> few rounds and they faltered and fell back. I thought we had licked them
> quickly and easily, but I soon saw my mistake.[13]

They attacked the Confederate position again, and penetrated the line in a few spots. But the Confederates had arranged their defending troops so they provided interlocking fields of fire. The main attack lasted only about eight minutes, with nearly eight thousand Union soldiers falling. It was the bloodiest charge of the war, even more than Pickett's charge at Gettysburg. By nightfall the Confederates had won a decisive victory over the North's superior numbers.

Controversy arose over the Union forces retreating and leaving their wounded on the battlefield, without attempting to retrieve them until two days later. Maj. Jedediah Hotchkiss, Stonewall Jackson's famous cartographer, stated: "Grant delayed sending a flag of truce to General Lee for this purpose because it would amount to an admission that he had been beaten on the 3d of June. It now seems incredible that he should, for a moment, have supposed that any other view could be taken of that action."[14]

The numbers showed that Grant lost over 10,000 men in the battle. Lee's army probably sustained a loss of less than 1500.[15] The Union losses were suppressed for a few days to prevent major problems at the Republican nominating convention, which would nominate Abraham Lincoln as its presidential candidate. But when finally disclosed, the high number of Union casualties at Cold Harbor "...produced a shudder in the North, intensified the peace movement and the opposition to Lincoln, and created in Union ranks an impression of reckless insanity in their commander..."[16] Casualties in the 30th Battalion were not heavy, but show the unit was definitely involved in the major portion of the action:

30th Battalion Virginia. Sharpshooters, CSA
Casualties: Battle of Cold Harbor, Virginia
May 31–June 3, 1864

	MWIA	WIA	MIA	CAPT	Totals:
Companies:					
A		4	1	3	8
B	1	3			4
C		4			4
D		3			3
E		3			3
F		1			1
	=====	=====	=====	=====	=====
Totals:	1	18	1	3	23

One of the Union attacks at the Battle of Cold Harbor, Va., June 3, 1864. Frank Leslie's *Illustrated* Newspaper

Abbreviations:
MWIA – Mortally wounded in action
WIA – Wounded in action
MIA – Missing in action
CAPT – Captured

On the night of June 3rd, Breckrinridge's Division, including Wharton's Brigade and the 30th Battalion Sharpshooters was relieved and replaced by other regiments.

On June 28, Col. J. Lyle Clark was sent to the hospital and then was given a sick-leave.[17] Since Clark remained either in the hospital or on sick leave through October, James Conrad Peters probably never saw him again.

The battalion was not to have a much-needed rest, however. On July 6 or 7 the men were ordered to march to Richmond. While there, the Union forces in the Virginia Valley under Generals Crook and Averell joined forces and began attacking towns along the valley. The 30th Battalion and the remainder of Wharton's Brigade marched to Lynchburg and camped near there. The battalion finally got a short rest during the middle of the month. On the 15th or 16th the battalion had a skirmish with Union troops. The men then traveled to the vicinity of Salem. During the first week of July

the men crossed the Potomac River and went into camp near Sharpsburg, Maryland. While passing through Harper's Ferry, West Virginia some of Breckinridge's command skirmished with the Union forces holding Maryland Heights. For the next few days they marched through parts of Maryland and Pennsylvania. John Schowen related that the battalion then "... marched to Fredrick City, a most beautiful little town and surrounded with beautiful country."[18]

On July 9, the Confederate Cavalry of John McCausland encountered breastworks flanked by two block-houses at the Monocacy Junction of the B & O Railroad near Frederick City, Maryland. Gen. Jubal Early ordered Breckinridge to bring his division, including Wharton's Brigade to their assistance. Entrenched at the junction were approximately 7,000 Union troops under Maj. Gen. Lew Wallace. Part of this force was the 14th New Jersey, the 8th Illinois Cavalry, the 10th Vermont, with other regiments from Ohio and Pennsylvania. Gen. Breckinridge immediately sent Gen. Gordon's Division into the fight. The degree of engagement of our men of the 30th Battalion is unclear. We do know that Wharton's Brigade had originally been positioned near the crossing of the Frederick Road over Ballenger Creek, and north of the B & O Railroad tracks. Some sources state that Wharton's Brigade was held in reserve and did not see action.[19] Schowen and others, however, state that they did see action that day. He stated that they drove back the enemy, killing a great many and capturing 700 prisoners.[20] Brig. Gen. Thomas Smith, commanding Smith's Brigade which fought alongside Wharton, was mortally wounded in the battle.

Confederate Brig. Gen. William N. Pendleton, Chief of Artillery, gave a concise report of the battle:

> Encountering little resistance on any part of the route, General Early's forces crossed the Potomac into Maryland, at Shepherdstown, on July 5 and 6. On the morning of the 9th they advanced upon Fredericktown. The enemy had evacuated that place, but was found in force on the line of the Monocacy a mile or two to the east, the railroad bridge and the ford below, on the Georgetown road, being the principal points of demonstration. Here a number of our guns were judiciously posted to bear upon the opposite side and operated with great effect, when McCausland's cavalry and Gordon's infantry, having crossed the stream, attacked the enemy and were met by him in line of battle at right angles to the river. Taken in flank and reverse by our artillery, the enemy's line immediately gave way and was soon routed and driven from the ford and bridge. The victory was complete.[21]

Even though a Confederate victory, the Battle of Monocacy would become known as "the battle that saved Washington and mayhap the Union."[22] Some believe that by delaying Early's advancing army by a day or day and a half, Washington was better fortified, and Early therefore did not capture the city after marching there on July 11. Some of the men of the 30th Battalion were in the rear guarding prisoners, so it is not known if they actually got to see the defenses at the outskirts of the city. On the 14th the Confederates recrossed the Potomac and rested near Upperville.

The next few weeks saw the men of the 30th Battalion marching through the Shenandoah Valley, near the towns of Kernstown and Strasburg. On July 24 the Con-

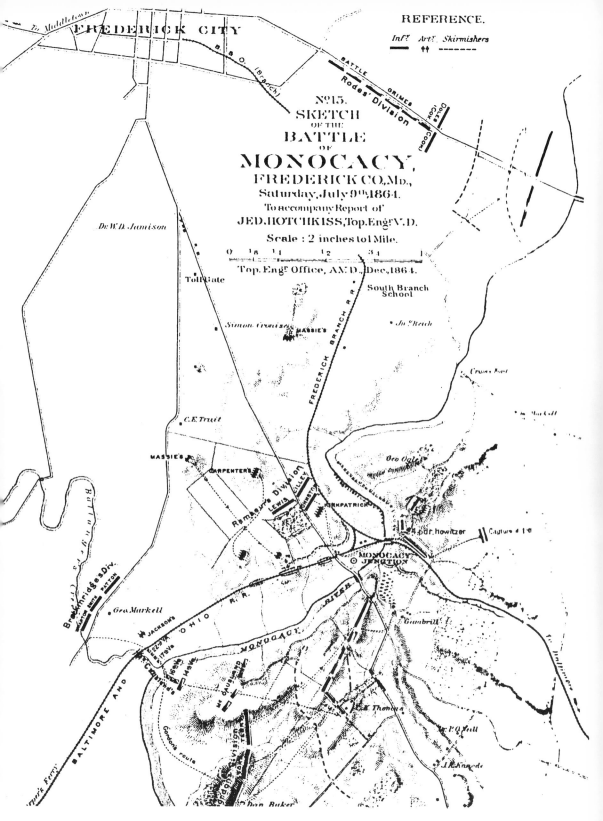

Map of Monocacy, MD., battlefield from Official Records Atlas.
Position of Wharton's Brigade, including 30th Battalion Sharpshooters
is north of B&O Railroad at lower left.

federates battled with the Union forces of Averell and Crook above Kernstown. The Confederate troops drove the retreating Yankees through Winchester and on to Bunker Hill.

The brigade marched toward Martinsburg, West Virginia where a formal inspection of troops was held. The first few days of August found the men of the 30th Battalion in the vicinity of Harper's Ferry and Shepherdstown. The men spent the last days of August and the first week of September in camp near Bunker Hill. The battalion served as pickets off and on until the 17th of September.

What Gen. Jubal Early did on the 18th of September was probably a blunder, but wisdom of hindsight is always twenty-twenty. He received word that Union repair crews were repairing the B & O Railroad at Martinsburg. Instead of securing a strong defensive position in the Valley, Early divided his army, sending a large part to Martinsburg to threaten the railroad. Therefore on the evening of the 18th of September, Early's troops were spread out as follows: his cavalry was at Martinsburg, Gordon's Division at Bunker Hill, Gen. Rodes on the way to Stephenson's Depot, Wharton's Brigade along with King's Battery was already at Stephenson's, and Ramseur's Division with Nelson's Battery was across the Berryville Pike east of Winchester.[23]

Union Gen. Phil Sheridan, upon learning of this division of Early's forces, ordered an immediate advance against Ramseur.

John Schowen, of Company F of the battalion, related the next morning's happenings as follows: "Skirmishing continuously on our line until the 17th when we went on picket. The morning of the 18th the drive commenced and the Yankees commenced firing just at daylight. They soon massed their forces and charged our lines very heavy firing all day."[24]

As soon as Gen. Early heard of the contact, he immediately ordered Gordon's Division to support Ramseur. As a general engagement developed, he then quickly ordered Rodes and Breckinridge to hurry in support of the other Confederates troops. By six a.m., Gen. George Custer and his Union cavalry had attacked some of the Rebel

Third Battle of Winchester, Va. Frank Leslie's *Illustrated* Newspaper

works, pushing them back. His Michigan Brigade encountered Confederates defending the crossing of the Opequon. At the ford of the Opequon were the 22nd Virginia Cavalry, and some of Wharton's Brigade acting as skirmishers. Probably the part of Wharton's Brigade that defended the ford was the 30th Battalion. The Union force pushed on through these Confederate defenders.

About ten a.m. Wharton's men and King's Battery skirmished with Wesley Merritt's Union Division while advancing toward the main action. With all the fighting in the morning, Wharton's Brigade did not arrive at Winchester until about two p.m.[25] The men of Wharton's Brigade were placed on the Confederate right flank alongside Ramseur's Division. They were hardly in place when they were ordered to the opposite flank, and were just in position when Union Gen. George Crook attacked. By four o'clock Crook and Gen. Torbert were simultaneously attacking Early's left flank. As the Confederate line was at right angles with the Martinsburg Pike, its flank was exposed to Crook, who was advancing between Wharton and Gordon. By five p.m., the Confederates were forced into a giant L-shaped line just east of town. Wharton with the remainder of Breckenridge's troops, and Gordon, facing north occupied the base, while Grimes and Ramseur, facing east extended the front.[26] Wharton and Gordon's men delivered a destructive fire into the Union forces, but on they came. Soon a major advance by the Union Sixth and Nineteenth Corps was pushing the men of Ramseur's and Rode's Divisions steadily back to Winchester. Finally the whole Confederate line was retreating. The Confederates fell back to some old breastworks that gave temporary shelter. But the effort to maintain the line did not last; the Union cavalry charged the left flank of the Confederate line, and a general retreat through Winchester was underway. "Old Jube" Early had no choice but to order a general withdrawal. Night found Gen. Sheridan's Union troops in full possession of Winchester, which had changed hands 73 times during the war. A Union infantry pursuit was not attempted, and Ramseur, by keeping his troops somewhat organized, covered the retreat.

Nevertheless, in this last attack the Confederates lost many men who were captured by the Union troops. Wharton's Brigade and the 30th Battalion had been overrun. James Conrad Peters and many of his compatriots were captured, again.

30th Battalion Virginia. Sharpshooters, CSA
Casualties: 3rd Battle of Winchester, Virginia
Sept. 19, 1864

Companies:	KIA	WIA	MIA	CAPT	Totals:
A	1	2		14	17
B		1		11	12
C		5		4	9
D				7	7
E	1	1		8	10
F		4		15	19
F & S		1			1
	======	======	======	======	======
Totals:	2	14	0	59	75

Abbreviations:
KIA – Killed in action
MWIA – Mortally wounded in action
WIA – Wounded in action
MIA – Missing in action
F & S – Field and staff officers
CAPT – Captured

30th Battalion Va. Sharpshooters, CSA
Casualties: Shenandoah Valley Campaign
May to September, 1864

	KIA	MWIA	WIA	MIA	CAPT	Totals
Battles:						
New Market	2	6	33	7		48
Cold Harbor		1	18	1	3	23
Winchester	2		14		59	75
Fisher's Hill			1		4	5
Kernstown	1		4			5
	====	=====	====	====	=====	=====
Totals:	5	7	70	8	66	156

Abbreviations:
KIA – Killed in action
MWIA – Mortally wounded in action
WIA – Wounded in action
MIA – Missing in action
CAPT – Captured

John Schowen related: "Brigade fell back to Winchester, their firing was effective. They drove us back killing and capturing several of our men."[27] The next day the Confederates fell back to Fisher's Hill where they would make another stand. But James Peters and his captured compatriots now faced the prospect of a Union prisoner of war camp. James must have remembered his first terrible experience at Camp Douglas. He no doubt wondered what this capture would bring and would he survive this imprisonment. Sometime in the previous months James Conrad Peters had been promoted to the rank of sergeant.

Reports Relating to the 3rd Battle of Winchester

Hdqrs. Third Brig., First Div., Sixth Army Corps,
[Winchester, Virginia.,] September 22, 1864

Lieut. Col. J. W. Forsyth,
    Chief of Staff:
....The Confederate prisoners at present in charge of the provost-marshal are being forwarded, guarded by Colonel Currie's brigade, of the Nineteenth Corps, to Harper's Ferry. The dead of both sides have all been buried, with the exception of a few, and details are at present at work collecting and interring them....

Very respectfully,

O. EDWARDS,
Colonel, Commanding Post.[28]

Winchester, Virginia., *September 19, 1864 — 7:30 p.m.*

Lieutenant-General Grant:

I have the honor to report that I attacked the forces of General Early on the Berryville pike at the crossing of Opequon Creek, and after a most stubborn and sanguinary engagement, which lasted from early in the morning until 5 o'clock in the evening, completely defeated him, and, driving him through Winchester, captured about 2,500 prisoners, 5 pieces of artillery, 9 army flags, and most of their wounded. The rebel General Rodes and General Gordon were killed, and three other general officers wounded. Most of the enemy's wounded and all their killed fell into our hands. Our losses are severe, among them General D. A. Russell, commanding division in the Sixth Corps, who was killed by a cannon-ball. Generals Upton, Mciontosh, and Chapman are wounded. I cannot yet tell our losses. The conduct of the officers and men was most superb. They charged and carried every position taken up by the rebels from the Opequon Creek to Winchester. The enemy were strong in number and very obstinate in their fighting. I desire to mention to the lieutenant-general commanding the army the gallant conduct of Generals Wright, Crook, Emory, Torbert, and the officers and men under their command; to them the country is indebted for this handsome victory. A more detailed report will be forwarded.

P. H. SHERIDAN,
Major-General[29]

HEADQUARTERS VALLEY DISTRICT,
New Market, October 9, 1864.

GENERAL: In advance of a detailed report I have determined to give you an informal account of the recent disasters to my command, which I have not had leisure to do before.

On the 17th of September I moved two divisions [Rodes' and Gordon's] from Stephensons Depot, where they, together with Breckinridges division, were encamped (Ramseur being at Winchester to cover the road from Berryville), to Bunker Hill, and on the 18th I moved Gordon's division, with a part of Lomax's cavalry, to Martinsburg, to thwart efforts that were reported to be making to repair the Baltimore and Ohio Railroad. This expedition was successful, and the bridge over Back Creek was burned by a brigade of cavalry sent there. On the evening of the 18th Rodes was moved back to Stephenson's Depot and Gordon to Bunker Hill, with orders to start at daylight to return to his camp at Stephenson's Depot, which place he reached at a very early hour next morning. About the time of Gordon's arrival on that morning firing was heard in Ramseur's front, and now a report reached me that the enemy's cavalry had appeared on the Berryville road. I ordered Rodes, Gordon, and Breckinridge to have their divisions under arms ready to move to Ramseur's assistance, and rode to his position to ascertain the extent and character of the demonstration. On getting there I found Ramseur's division in line of battle, and the enemy evidently advancing with his whole force. The other divisions were immediately ordered up and the trains all put in motion for their security. Rodes and Gordon arrived just before the enemy commenced advancing a heavy force on Ramseur's left for the purpose of overwhelming him, and when their columns commenced advancing on Ramseur I attacked them with Rodes' and Gordon's divisions, and drove them back, with great slaughter, the artillery doing most splendid service, Braxton's battalion, driving back with canister a heavy force, before which Evans' brigade, of Gordon's division, which was on the left, had given way. This brigade was now rallied, and Battle's brigade coming to its assistance, the enemy was pushed back a considerable distance, and we were successful. Breckinridge's division did not arrive for some time, because General Breckinridge had moved it out after my order to him to drive back some of the enemy's cavalry which was crossing the Opequon, and I sent for him again, and he came up in the afternoon before the enemy had made any further attack; but as he reported the enemy's cavalry advancing on the road from Charlestown, by Brucetown and Stephenson's Depot, I ordered one of his brigades to the left on that road, and directed General Fitz Lee to take charge of all the cavalry on that flank (my left) and check the enemy's cavalry, and moved the other two brigades of Breckinridge's division toward the right, where our forces were weakest and the enemy was making demonstrations in force. Breckinridge was scarcely in position before our cavalry on the left was discovered coming back in great confusion, followed by the enemy's, and Breckinridge's force was ordered to the left to repel this cavalry force, which had gotten in rear of my left, and this, with the assistance of the artillery, he succeeded in doing; but as soon as the firing was heard in rear of our left flank the infantry commenced falling back along the whole line, and it was very difficult to stop them. I succeeded, however, in stopping enough of them in the old rifle pits constructed by General Johnston to arrest the progress of the enemy's infantry, which commenced advancing again when the confusion in our ranks was discovered, and could have still won the day if our cavalry would have stopped the enemy's; but so overwhelming was the battle, and so demoralized was a larger part of ours, that no assistance was received from it. The enemy's cavalry again charged around my left flank, and the men began to give way again, so that it was necessary for me to retire through the town. Line of battle was formed on the north side of the town, the command reorganized, and we then turned back deliberately to Newtown, and the next day to Fisher's.

We lost three pieces of artillery, two of which had been left with the cavalry on the left, and the other was lost because the horses were killed and it could not be brought off.

In this fight I had already defeated the enemy's infantry, and could have continued to do so, but the enemy's very great superiority in cavalry and the comparative inefficiency of ours turned the scale against us.

In this battle the loss in the infantry and artillery was: Killed, 226; wounded, 1,567; missing, 1,818; total, 3,611.

There is no full report of the cavalry, but the total loss in killed and wounded from September 1 to October 1 is: Killed, 60; wounded, 288; total, 348. But many were captured, though a good many are missing as stragglers, and a number of them reported missing in the infantry were not captured, but are stragglers and skulkers. Wharton's (Breckinridge's) division lost six colors, and Rodes' division captured two. Rodes' division made a very gallant charge, and he was killed conducting it.

I fell back to Fisher's Hill, as it was the only place where a stand could be made, and I was compelled to detach Fitz Lee's cavalry to the Luray Valley to hold the enemy's cavalry in check should it advance up that valley. The enemy's loss at Winchester was very heavy. Doctor McGuire has received a letter from a member of his family who states that 5,800 of the enemy's wounded were brought to the hospital at Winchester, and that the total wounded was between 6,000 and 7,000; and a gentleman who passed over the field says that the number of killed was very large. Sheridan's medical director informed one of our surgeons left at Woodstock that the number of wounded in hospital at Winchester was the same as stated in the letter to Doctor McGuire, and I am satisfied from what I saw that the enemy's loss was very heavy. The enemy's infantry force was nearly, if not quite, three times as large as mine, and his cavalry was very much superior, both in numbers and equipment. This I have learned from intelligent persons who have seen the whole of both forces.

I posted my troops in line at Fisher's Hill with the hope of arresting Sheridan's progress, but my line was very thin, and having discovered that the position could be flanked, as is the case with every position in the Valley, I had determined to fall back on the night of the 22d, but late that evening a heavy force was moved under cover of the woods on the left and drove back the cavalry there posted, and got in the rear of my left flank, and when I tried to remedy this the infantry got into a panic and gave way in confusion, and I found it impossible to rally it. The artillery behaved splendidly, both on this occasion and at Winchester. I had to order the guns to be withdrawn, but the difficulties of the ground were such that twelve guns were lost because they could not be gotten off.

The loss in the infantry and artillery was 30 killed, 210 Wounded, and 995 missing; total, 1,235. I have been able to get no report of the loss in the cavalry, but it was slight. Very many of the missing in the infantry took to the mountains. A number of them have since come in and others are still out. The enemy did not capture more than 400 or 500, but I am sorry to say many men threw away their arms.

The night favored our retreat, and by next morning the commands were pretty well organized. At Mount Jackson next day I halted and drove back a force of cavalry which was pursuing, and then moved to Rude's Hill, where I halted until the enemy's infantry came up next day and was trying to flank me, when I moved off in line of battle for eight miles, occasionally halting to check the enemy. This continued until nearly sundown, when I got a position at which I checked the enemy's further progress for that day, and then moved under cover of night toward Port Republic to unite with Kershaw. After doing this I drove a division of cavalry from my front at Port Republic, and then moved to Waynesborough, where two divisions under Torbert were destroying the bridge, and drove them away; and after remaining there one day I moved to the vicinity of Mount Crawford, where I awaited the arrival of Rosser's brigade to take the offensive, but before it arrived the enemy was discovered to be falling back on the morning of the 6th. I immediately commenced following the enemy, and arrived here on the 7th, and have been waiting to ascertain whether Sheridan intends crossing the Blue Ridge before moving farther.

Respectfully,

J. A. EARLY,

Lieutenant-General.

General R. E. LEE.[30]

Map of Point Lookout made late 1863 or early 1864. Confederate prison compound housing the tents and cookhouses is the large enclosure in the upper right quadrant of the map. Courtesy Point Lookout State Park

46A

1. Light house.	7. Chapel.	13. Ward E.
2. Dining room & kitchen.	8. Reservoir.	14. E. L. Donnellys Stores.
3. Hospital Headquarters.	9. Circle of wards.	15. Dead house.
4. Baggage house.	10. Ward C	16. Sisters' quarters.
5. Reading room.	11. " D.	17. Wharf & Post Com. buildings.
6. Half Diet kitchen.	12. " F	18. Ice house.

POINT
VIEW OF HAMMOND GEN: HOS

34. Line dividing Hospt. fr. Miltary.	40. Office of Com. of Musters

19. Laundry,
20. Guard quarters,
21. Hospt. Com. & Clerks Mess room,
22. Old hotel — wards A & B,
23. Bakery,
24. Commissary building.

25. Ward I.
26.   "   K.
27.   "   G.
28. Rear of Ferguson boarding house
29. Allens boarding house,
30. Spauld'ng's photograph gallery.

31. Qrs. of
    Surg. K
32. Qurs. of A
    in charge
33. Qurs. of
    charge

9. Qurs. of Col. Bailey 2nd, N. H. V.   54. Qurs. of Union recruits from rebel   59. Burying ground
   Camp of 2nd N. H. V.   prisoners.   60. Small pox hospital.

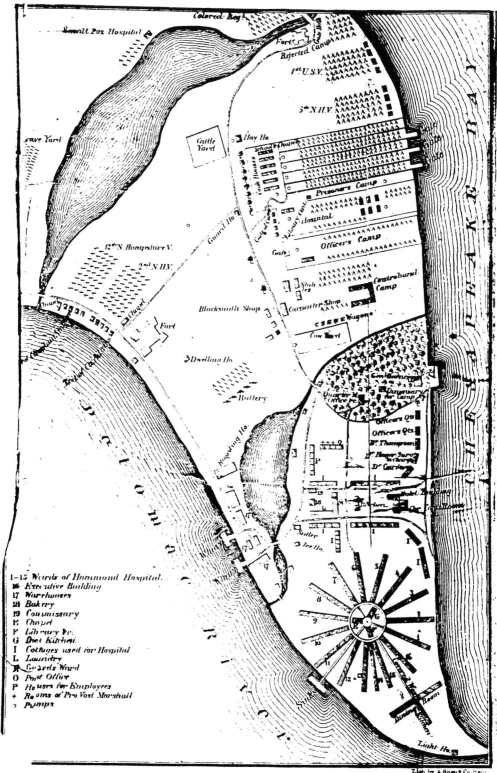

HOSPITAL & MILITARY PRISON AT POINT LOOKOUT.

By Rev. A. B. Cross, U. S. Christian Committee

Chapter IX

A POW Again

Point Lookout, Maryland Prison:
"June 3, 1865: If it were not for Hope, how could we live in a place like this?"
Unknown Confederate soldier[1]

On Monday, Sept. 26, 1864, James Conrad Peters arrived at the Point Lookout, Maryland prison compound with about 800 other prisoners.[2] They were transported by train through Harper's Ferry, West Virginia to Baltimore. (The B & O Railroad ran from Winchester, through Harper's Ferry, to Baltimore.) Most of the prisoners were then conveyed by steamboat from Baltimore down Chesapeake Bay to the wharf at Point Lookout. Another prisoner who had been at Point Lookout for some time, Sgt. Bartlett Y. Malone of Company H, 6th North Carolina Infantry, mentioned their arrival in his diary: "Sept. 26: 800 prisoners arrived at this point belonging to Erleys command captured clost to Winchester."[3] Another 500 prisoners arrived the next day. These arrivals brought the total of prisoners then at Point Lookout to almost 9,000.

Point Lookout had been constructed on a narrow peninsula in Maryland where the Chesapeake Bay and the Potomac River converge. It was at the extreme southern tip of St. Mary's County, about seventy miles southeast of Washington. The area was flat with some marsh and was barely above water. It had originally been built as a 1,400-bed hospital, but following the Battle of Gettysburg in 1863, it was modified to handle prisoners. The camp was officially named Camp Hammond or Camp Hoffman, but became universally known as Point Lookout and to the prisoners as "The Point." It was described by another prisoner, Rev. Malachi Bowden, as:

It was enclosed by a tall, upright plank fence, about 15 feet high. At the top, along the outside of the planks, was a bridge or walk extending around the prison. A man standing upon this walk could be seen from the inside of the prison from his waist line up. Along the parapet, at short intervals, were placed guards of Negro soldiers. The only protection we had from the weather was an ordinary army tent.[4]

These army tents were the first major difference between the Point and Camp Douglas that James would have noticed. There were no barrack buildings as there were at Camp Douglas, but there were wooden cookhouses. The tents were mostly bell-shaped and were supposedly the culls that had been rejected by the Union Army. It is possible that the high plank fence enclosing the prison compound was still under construction on the day James and his fellow prisoners arrived.

Another prisoner further described the interior of the Point as it appeared in the fall of 1863:

The camp was laid off in divisions, with streets between like a town. After I had been there about three months, the eleventh division was formed. These divisions were composed of ten companies, lettered like a regiment....Each division had a Confederate surgeon.....[5]

During October of 1864 the prison population exceeded 10,000. Bartlett Malone mentioned that "Ther is about 10,000 prisoners here at this time."[6] On October 23 Br. Gen James Barnes, the post commandant, requested more tents. Barnes was the post commandant during the entire period that James Peters was confined at Point Lookout. Major Allen G. Brady was Provost Marshall during the same period.

In November, with winter coming on, there was a shortage of blankets and clothing. Major Brady reported that one-third of the tents housing the prisoners was unfit for use. In his report of Nov 1864, Brady stated that many of the men were barefoot for want of shoes. Both Major Brady and other officers petitioned the War Department to have wooden barracks constructed for the prisoners. Their request was denied and the tents would become the only shelter for the prisoners during the harsh winter to come.

Rev. J. B. Traywick, who was at Point Lookout the same time as James Conrad Peters, spoke of that winter:

> I have heard men pray to be made sick that the appetite might be taken away. The prisoners being so poorly clad, and the Point so much exposed to cold, it caused them great suffering. Every intensely cold night from four to seven prisoners would freeze to death. Almost no wood was furnished. About a cord of green pine to one thousand men for five days. It was a mockery.[7]

Bartlett Y. Malone recorded that on the 18th of Feb., 1865 it was so cold that a man's breath would freeze on his beard going from the tent to the cookhouse.

There is no question that the use by the Union commanders of newly recruited African Americans, often recent slaves, was a factor in promoting animosity at the prison. The Confederates usually reacted with contempt toward these guards, and these feelings were frequently returned by the black soldiers. To further aggravate this naturally tense situation Major Brady sometimes enjoyed galloping his horse through crowds of prisoners, trampling those unable to get out of the way. This activity was referred to by some of the prisoners as "Brady's Sunday exercise."[8]

The punishment for trying to escape was cruel. Those who were caught were strung up to a pole by the thumbs, with the tips of their toes just touching the ground. Sometimes the men would lapse into unconsciousness, and have to be cut down.

Just as at Camp Douglas, smallpox became a large problem at Point Lookout. A separate hospital to treat the soldiers who contracted the disease was constructed north of the camp. The various buildings of the regular camp hospital, known as the Hammond Hospital, were located on the end of the peninsula and were positioned like the spokes on a wheel. On Jan. 26, 1865, there were so many sick soldiers that the inspector of prisons, Br. Gen. H. W. Wessells, instructed Gen. Barnes to use prison labor to construct three additional hospital buildings.[9]

The food received by prisoners, both North and South, was always a point of bitter feelings and disgust. A Pvt. Boseworth, captured at Cedar Creek a month after James Conrad Peters described it thusly:

Our rations in the morning consisted of a boiled piece of fat bacon about three inches square for breakfast. At noon we were given a bowl of 'bean soup,' which occasionally had a few beans in it, and a small loaf of bread, which must last us two days. Some of the men were so starved that they would eat the whole loaf at once; but I found it was better to save part of it. One of our pet amusements after a dinner like this was to describe the good dinners that we enjoyed at home, to talk of the white cloths on the table and the big dishes of fried chicken and pie that were sure to be on mother's table. O how we longed for food![10]

Point Lookout State Park sign marking the spot of the smallpox hospital. It stood well north of the other buildings at the prison.

Between March and May, 1865, the prison population grew to over 20,000 making Point Lookout the largest Union prison.[11] On March 15, 1865, James Conrad Peters appears on a roll of POWs as paroled from Point Lookout and transferred to Aiken's Landing, Virginia for exchange. He was one of 1,046 prisoners exchanged on that date. James probably departed the Point on the flag-of-truce boat *New York*, which left the wharf on March 17. Once again James had survived a Union prison camp.

Also during March two members of James' sharpshooters battalion died at Point Lookout. On March 18, 1865, only three days after James was exchanged, Pvt. William T. Ross of Co A died of pneumonia. Pvt. Ross had been captured with James Peters on Sept. 19, 1864. On March 24, 1865, Pvt. Leroy Wood of Co D, died at Point Lookout of measles and was buried in the camp cemetery.[12]

Plaque showing the name of Leroy Wood of Co. D, 30th Battalion Va. Sharpshooters as one of the 3,384 Confederate soldiers buried in the Point Lookout Confederate Cemetery. Point Lookout State Park, MD

James Conrad Peters passed down only one piece of oral history that has been preserved. This story involved an incident that occurred while he was incarcerated at Point Lookout. The following story was related to the grandfather of the editor by James, and starts with Peters befriending another prisoner named "Fog" Perdue. These two friends no doubt made a strange-looking pair, as Peters was only about 5 foot 6 inches tall, and Perdue was "well over six foot." These two friends, like hundreds of other prisoners at the Point, took turns stealing rations from some of the guards and dividing this contraband among their fellow prisoners. Peters related that one of the Union guards caught the pair during one of their forays, and stuck Peters in the hindparts with a bayonet. This enraged Perdue, who grabbed half a brick he had been hiding, and hit the guard in the side of the head. The guard supposedly died immediately, but Perdue and Peters were able to return to their tent without being caught. This story is so similar to the following incident, documented by another prisoner at Point Lookout, that there is no doubt that it occurred. This prisoner was Rev. J. B. Traywick:

"The greatest cruelty perpetuated while I was in prison was on thirty-two inmates of one of the cook-houses. At the side of the prison, next to the gate, was located a number of long cook and eating-houses, where all the cooking except baking was done. There was only a street or roadway between these houses and the stockade where the guards walked continually. Between two of these houses, a little nearer one than the other, one of the guards fell from the parapet and was found dead. A contusion was on his head and a piece of brick near him. This discovery took place about sunset. No one saw who hit him.

"The following night after taps, when every prisoner was in bed, a file of soldiers rushed into the nearest cook-house to the scene and hurried the thirty-two inmates out in the night. The weather was intensely cold—thermometer below zero. They had on nothing but shirt and drawers—two of them had on socks. They were placed in a block-house which had a door and a hole a few inches wide, without food, water or fire. They were told that one of them killed the negro guard, possibly all of them knew of it, and when the fact was so made known, then all the others could go back to their quarters, but if they did not come out and confess who killed the guard that the day following the next had been fixed as the time when all thirty-two of them would be shot. So in that bitter weather these innocent helpless men (not all men, for two of them were boys) passed that fearful night and next day in the block building, where they were continually jeered at through the little window by the negro guards who were off duty, they telling the suffering prisoners how delighted they would be to see them shot.

"The awful hours rolled on, another night of indescribable suffering passed away, and the day of execution has come. To many of these men a quick death was to be preferred to the slow and cruel death they were then passing. The hour for the execution arrives. All the troops, mostly negroes, off guard on the Point were formed into the hollow square. The thirty-two almost naked, freezing, starving men were marched out in line into the hollow square. Major Brady, with the audacity of the wolf before eating the lamb, proceeded to ask each man if he knew who killed the guard. As he proceeded he received a very positive no from the heroic boys first, and then from the brave men. He had not gone far, however, when an alarm was heard in the direction of the gate. Four or five men were seen coming on horseback at full speed and yelling at the top of their voices. It was an officer who had found a young man, a prisoner and employ in the next cook-house, who could tell them something about who killed the guard.

"But we must go back one day in the narrative. During that day of cruel mocking there was one kind man who visited the suffering prisoners. He was a commissioned officer and a Mason. Among the thirty-two prisoners there was but one Mason, and he gave a signal which will stir the deepest emotions of a brother. This officer lost no time, but set to work to ferret out the cause of the death of the guard. Major Brady, unfeeling monster as he was, attempted to find out the cause by torturing innocent men.

"Of course the proceedings were stayed until the young man was heard from. He was placed on a box to testify, but he could not do this until Major Brady had indulged in some silly, irrelevant questions. He, however, stated that on the evening the guard was killed he was at the wood-pile gathering some chips for the fire when he was hit on the leg by the brick. Smarting with pain he threw the brick back and hit the guard on the head, and he fell off the parapet. Whether, said the young man, the brick or the whiskey in the guard caused the fall and death he could not say; for, said he, the guard was drunk that afternoon. Then the young man added, I am sorry that I did not know that you were bestowing this cruelty on these men, for I should have come forward and made known these things.

"The thirty-two were immediately sent back to their quarters, where they were clothed and fed, but three of them died soon after from this exposure, and most of them had impaired health. As for the young man, he was never punished for what he did, but in a few weeks he was acting courier for Major Brady in the prison."[13]

Rev. Traywick was paroled from Point Lookout on February 18, 1865, one month before James Conrad Peters.

The only question remaining after comparing the two accounts of the same incident, is: was Fog Perdue the young man that Rev. Traywick said came forward and confessed to the killing, so that his fellow prisoners would not be shot? If so, James Conrad Peters was most likely one of the thirty-two prisoners questioned. The other fact that supports this story is that James Conrad Peters was a member of the Masons.

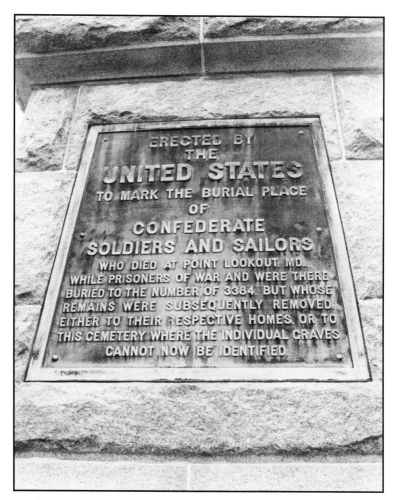

Plaque at Point Lookout Confederate Cemetery to the 3,384 Confederate soldiers who died at Point Lookout.

Monument at Point Lookout Confederate Cemetery, Point Lookout State Park, Md.

Only original surviving building of the Point Lookout prison. Edwin Beitzell, historian of Point Lookout, identified this building in 1971 as Mr. Spaulding's Photographic Gallery.

Chapter X
The War Finally Ends

The time between March 15, 1865, when James Conrad Peters was exchanged from Point Lookout, and the end of the Civil War was less than a month. With the surrender of Gen. Robert E. Lee and the Army of Northern Virginia on April 9, the war in the Virginias ended for the Confederate forces. Where James Peters was during this time period is unknown. He probably walked on foot from Aiken's Landing, Virginia to his home in Mercer County, now in West Virginia. The men of the Confederate infantry, including the sharpshooters battalions, did begin "the long walk home" when either paroled at Appomattox following the surrender, or when paroled from a northern prison. Only some of the cavalry were allowed to keep their horses. We do know that James was near Charleston, West Virginia on June 22, when he signed his parole papers. He gave his age as 26, his height as 5 foot 6 inches, complexion: dark, eyes: hazel and hair: dark. He was shown as a sergeant in Co. B, 30th Virginia Battalion of Infantry.[1]

Copy of James Conrad Peters' parole papers he signed on June 22, 1865 at Charleston, W.V. Notice his age was given as 26 years, height as 5'6", complexion: dark, eyes: hazel, and hair: dark.

Following the dated diary entries in the Peters diary is the following accounting of what equipment James Conrad Peters returned:

Returned to the
Southern Confederacy:

1 Saddle Blanket
1 Nose bag
1 Cartridge box & c
1 Curry comb & brush
1 circingle
1 Bridle & c
1 Shot gun

Since these items included those issued for a horseman, it is possible that these items were returned before James Peters left for Ft. Donelson. They could also have been returned when the unit was converted to an artillery battery in 1861.

On the last page of James Conrad Peters' diary is a small sketch of a Confederate flag with these words:

This Confederate
flag Oh long
may it wave
oer the land
of the Free and
the home of
the brave.

The terrible Civil War was finally over. James Conrad Peters had survived the terrible conditions on the battlefield only to have been captured twice and confined to two of the worst prison camps in the North. He had watched many of his compatriots die of wounds and disease. But he had endured. Now he would be returning home to his family and a new life.

No fault can be found with the Confederate soldier subsequent to the war....He at once discarded the implements of war for those of peace and began the battle for existence uncomplainingly with little on his side but an indomitable will.[2]

Chapter XI

A Peaceful Life at Mercer Salt Works

The Reconstruction following the end of the War was hard for the ex-Confederates. In the deep South, which was occupied by Union forces for several years, these returning soldiers were subjected to many humiliating experiences. While these men were allowed to wear what remnants of Confederate uniforms they had on their backs, all Confederate or other military buttons had to be removed. Horses that had been kept by the cavalrymen were confiscated if they had a "US" brand, even though the men pleaded that they were captured as "spoils of war" and were needed for the spring plowing. Since West Virginia came into the Union as a northern state during the War, the Reconstruction Period was not as harsh there. There were attempts, sometimes successful, to confiscate property of ex-Confederate officers as a result of legal proceedings brought against them for raids carried out during the War. "For most Southerners Lee's surrender did not mark the end of life but the beginning of a difficult period of readjustment to new conditions."[1] James Peters, being an ordinary foot soldier, was lucky enough to return home and begin a quiet life with his family.

Following the war, James Conrad Peters and his young family moved to Mercer Salt Works in Mercer County, West Virginia. This little settlement has a fascinating history. It was located at the junction of New River and Lick Creek in what is today Summers County, West Virginia. Prior to the formation of Summers County in 1871, the site was in Mercer County. Most histories refer to the actual salt works being located one-half mile above (or west) of the junction of Lick Creek and New River. The first commercial salt well was bored there in 1849 and known as the Jabez Anderson Salt Well. Horses supplied the power to bore the well and it was bored to a depth of 800 feet.[2] A small settlement grew up around the mill and the location gradually became the center of society in that area. People came to the works to buy their salt, coffee, have their meal and flour ground, pick up their mail, and to socialize. Following is a description of the salt producing process before the Civil War and what was located there:

> The salt manufacturing operation consisted of 8 drying pans, a furnace with a large smoke-stack and some auxiliary buildings that accompanied the salt extracting process. The salt brine was pumped from the ground by a steam engine to the drying pans. The bottoms of the pans were three-fourths inch thick and were cast iron. The sides were wooden. The forest in the vicinity of the works were denuded of their vegetation to fuel the furnace to operate the works.[3]

By 1852 a road connected the Salt Works with the outside world. Mr. Vawter's map dated Feb, 1852 shows the "Princeton & Red Sulphur Road" coming from the west, traveling down Lick Creek, past what he marked as the "Salt Well" and across New River. The road probably crossed the river at Shanklin's Ferry a little south of the Salt Works. The road then wound eastward into Monroe County and connected with the Giles, Fayette & Kanawha Turnpike near present-day Ballard, West Virginia. This turnpike had been completed in 1848 and ran north-south through Peterstown, Red Sulphur Springs, Beckley and Fayetteville.[4]

In November 1863, the land was sold under bond from William B. Crump to Anderson Shumate for $7,300 in Confederate money. Shumate brought suit after the War to recover the total in United States currency since during the War he "...didn't dare to refuse to accept it (Confederate currency) due to the prevailing sentiment in favor of the Confederacy in the New River Valley."[5] In 1868 the judgment was rendered in favor of Shumate.

During the Civil War, it was noted that the salt produced at the Salt Works was carried out on horseback.[6] The salt was important to the Confederacy as it was used to

James Conrad Peters and Polly Ann,
pictured at Mercer Salt Works.
Photo circa 1905-1910.

make saltpetre, an element of black powder. At various times during the War, Confederate units were sent to guard the Salt Works. Due to other seemingly more important missions, however, the Confederate units guarding the Salt Works were frequently absent. As a result, the Salt Works was attacked and burned by Union cavalry under command of Col. Rutherford B. Hayes on Aug. 10, 1862. His 23rd Ohio Regiment was encamped at Camp Green Meadows on the Bluestone River. Hayes dispatched the riders who rode fifty miles that night. "They reached the salt works at 2 a.m., found it going full blast, and it was burned out 'root and branch.'"[7] Miraculously there were no human casualties, although three horses were wounded. Hayes himself did not take actual part in the raid and never saw the Salt Works. There are no records of any of the homes in the area being burned or damaged in the raid.

At its peak after the War, the community consisted of a general store and post office, blacksmith shop, a one-room school, a large mill located at the falls and several homes. In 1871 there was only one frame house at Mercer Salt Works which was owned by the Shumates. The implication was that the other dwellings were built of logs. The first post office was established on Sept. 8, 1851 when it was in Mercer County, Virginia. It was discontinued Sept. 5, 1868 but reestablished Sept. 5, 1870. It was closed for the last time July 31, 1914. James C. Peters and his daughter Mary E. Peters were postmaster and postmistress at the Salt Works Postoffice at various times. In 1874 a voting precinct was established at the Salt Works.

It is difficult to determine exactly when James Peters and his family arrived at Mercer Salt Works. Summers County was not created until 1871, but even in the 1880

Historical marker near the site of Mercer Salt Works mentioning
the burning of the Salt Works on Aug. 10, 1862 by Union cavalry.

Earliest known map showing the location of the salt well at Mercer Salt Works. Map drawn by Mr. John Vawter in 1852 and showing the location was in Mercer County, Va., later Summers County, WV. Courtesy West Virginia State Archives

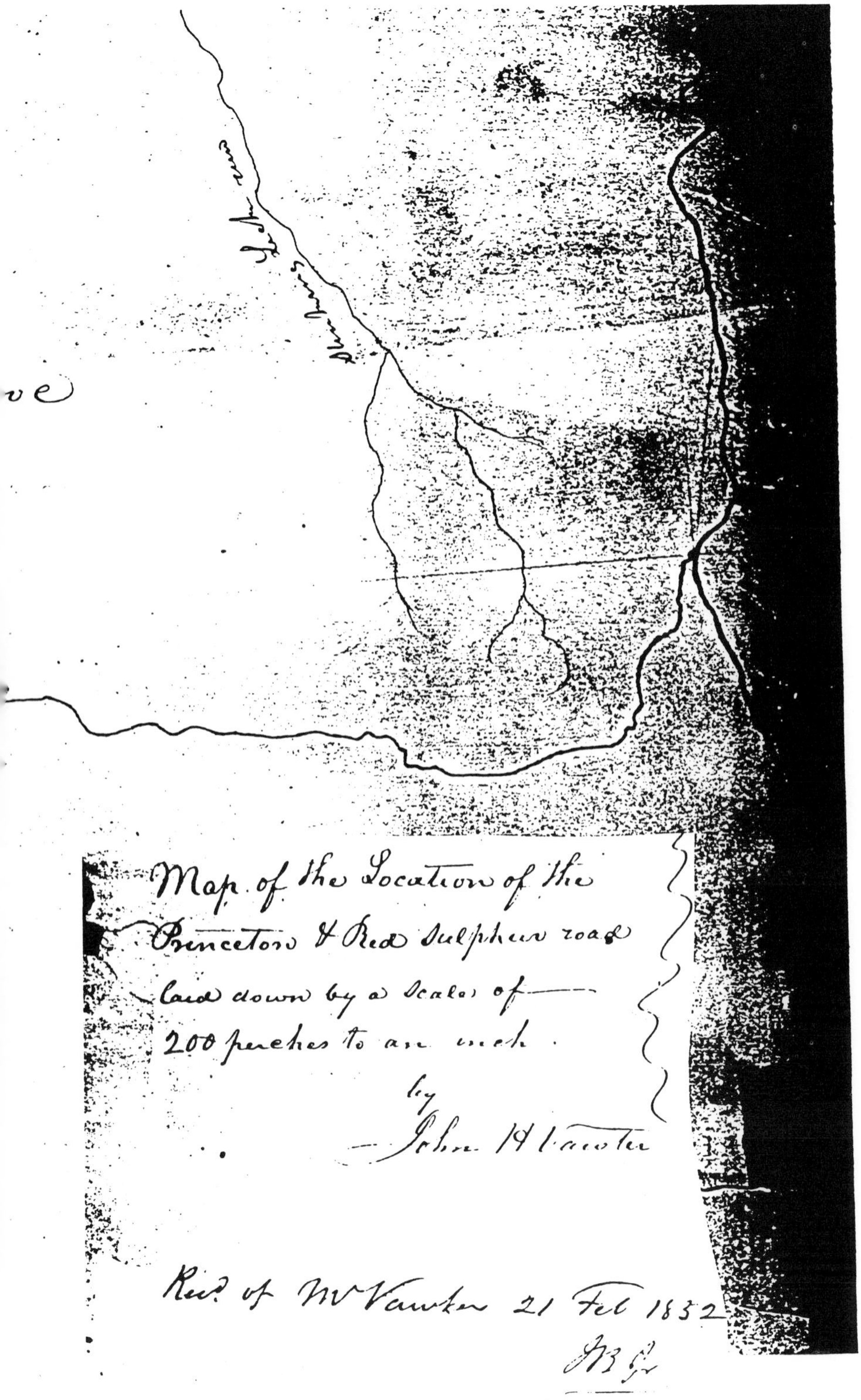

Map of the Location of the
Princeton & Red Sulphur road
laid down by a Scale of —
200 perches to an inch .

by

— John H Vawter

Rec.d of Mr Vawter 21 Feb 1852

Colton's 1855 map of Virginia.
One of the first maps to show the new state of West Virginia. Probably printed between June 1863 and January 1864. Jefferson and Berkeley counties, which would soon become part of West Virginia's eastern panhandle, were still part of Virginia. Courtesy Alderman Library, University of Virginia

The falls of Lick Creek near New River in Summers County, WV. The mill at Mercer Salt Works stood on the near side of the falls.

Geological Survey marker at the location of Mercer Salt Works, Summers County, WV.

Census of West Virginia, James and his family were still enumerated in the East River Dist. of Mercer County.[8] James's occupation was shown as farmer. Certainly they were at Mercer Salt Works well before 1890. In the 1900 census the family was enumerated as residing there on June 9, 1900.[9] In 1902 Peters purchased 1040 acres from Ballard P. Shumate, "...being 1040 acres inherited by party of the first part from his father Anderson Shumate."[10] The land was described as lying in Pipestem District of Summers County and beginning on the banks of New River and crossing Lick Creek. This deed took in the area of Mercer Salt Works. In this deed James C. Peters was referred to as guardian for two of his grandchildren: Annie L. and James M. Anderson. These were children of James's daughter, Mettie Burke Peters, who had married James D. Anderson, Jr. and had died in 1899.

Oral family history has passed down the following interesting story. Sometime after the Peters family moved to Mercer Salt Works, stories were circulated that the old mill was haunted. These stories related that anyone who ever stayed near the mill after dark was shook out of their wits by the sound of boards being sawed, and sometimes this sawing would continue all night. James Conrad finally set out to disprove these tales and with his old pistol and oil lamp he walked to the mill and waited for dark. After dark Peters began hearing noises and they did indeed sound like boards being vigorously sawed! Peters took his pistol and began searching for the source of the noises. He found nothing until he reached the dirt-floor cellar. In this old cellar salt had been barreled up from the Salt Works. Peters then saw the cause of the mysterious sounds: two barrels were turned over on the floor and a cow was licking at one of them, trying to get the last bit of salt. As the cow nudged one of the barrels, it would rub the metal rim of the other, producing the sound resembling that of raw boards being sawed. James C. Peters supposedly then moved his family into the old mill, changed the second floor into their living quarters, and lived there for many years.

Like his ancestors before him, James was a leader of his little community. He was justice of the peace from about 1898 to 1908 and was postmaster during that same period.[11] He also operated the general store at the Salt Works for a number of years. The Shumates actually owned the store and James operated it for them.

James Conrad Peters died at Mercer Salt Works on Jan. 9, 1911. James's obituary in the Hinton *Independent Herald* related that he died of Bright's Disease and that he was one of the well to do farmers of the area. Polly Ann died on Nov. 22, 1928. Both were buried in the cemetery that would become known as the Peters-Anderson Cemetery near the Salt Works. According to the Corps of Engineers records, James was buried in a concrete vault and

J. C. PETERS DEAD

J. C. Peters, one of the well to do farmers of this section, died last night at his home near Warford, this county. Mr. Peters has been sick for some time with Bright's Disease and his death was not unexpected. He is survived by his wife and a host of friends. The funeral will take place tomorrow afternoon and the interment will be at his home place.

Polly was buried in a steel vault.[12]

Mercer Salt Works was one of the locations that was abandoned in the 1950s when the Bluestone Dam was being planned. The backwater does not actually cover the site, but all the roads were cut off or abandoned. Today the foundations of two of the houses are all that remain of this once-thriving little community.

Even the people who had been buried near the Salt Works were not allowed to rest. When the Bluestone Dam was being built all the cemeteries judged to be below the projected water line of the lake were relocated. Initially the small cemetery known as the Peters-Anderson Cemetery where James Conrad Peters and his family were interred was not scheduled to be relocated by the Army Corps of Engineers. Corps of Engineers maps show the location of the cemetery as being about 1/4 mile from New River. About 1951 Florence B. Spangler and others petitioned the Corps to have the cemetery relocated due to access over the dirt roads becoming impossible. To relocate one of these cemeteries is truly an engineering feat. The Corps of Engineers first maps the layout of the original cemetery, even cataloging the unknown graves. Then they attempt to locate the next of kin of each of the marked graves. The next of kin is notified and given an opportunity to have the graves moved to a location of their choosing. If a next of kin cannot be located or that person does not desire to move the graves to a location of their choosing, then the Corps relocates the graves to another location in the area. In 1953, the Corps showed on their map of the Peters-Anderson Cemetery ten graves inside a "woven wire fence." Outside the fence were another seven graves that were unknown. It is possible these graves contain the remains of slaves from the area. There was a tradition in parts of the South that slaves were frequently buried "outside the fence" of family cemeteries. A note on the Corps of Engineers files states that: "Local information indicates that unknowns were apparently buried before 1866."[13] Of the ten graves inside the fence, notes on the list of interred showed that four members of the Peters family were moved to a location chosen by the next of kin, and four members of the Anderson family were moved to Resthaven Cemetery in Princeton, West Virginia. The notation for the four Peters family members reads "Nearest of kin signed permits agreeing to provide burial lots and to pay a reasonable extra cost, if any, for reinterment in Butler Cemetery near Tophet, W. Virginia."[14] Tophet is a small crossroads just across the Mercer County line only a few miles from the site of the original cemetery. The four graves moved to Tophet were James Conrad Peters, his wife Polly Ann Peters, and two of their daughters: Mary E. Peters and Edith R. Gore. Notes on the map show that the remaining graves, including the unknown graves outside the fence, were relocated to the Fairview Cemetery site at Peterstown. The two members of the Peters family relocated to the Peterstown Cemetery were Robert McNutt Peters (James Conrad's younger brother) and David T. Peters (a son of Robert McNutt Peters).

James Conrad Peters was a property appraiser, soldier, farmer, merchant, postmaster, and justice of the peace, but he is most remembered as a caring and sensitive patriarch. Near the turn of the twentieth century, one of his daughters was experiencing a failed marriage. True to form, James Peters hitched up a buckboard and rode alone over the hills of southern West Virginia in a driving rain to rescue his daughter. When the irate and drunken husband made serious threats to both James and his daughter, James quietly spoke only one sentence: "She's coming home now." Oral

Entrance to Butler Cemetery at Tophet, WV., where the Peters
family graves were relocated.

Headstones of Polly Ann and James Conrad Peters in the Butler Cemetery.

Peters-Anderson Cemetery *
Mercer Salt Works
Summers County, WV
ca. 1950

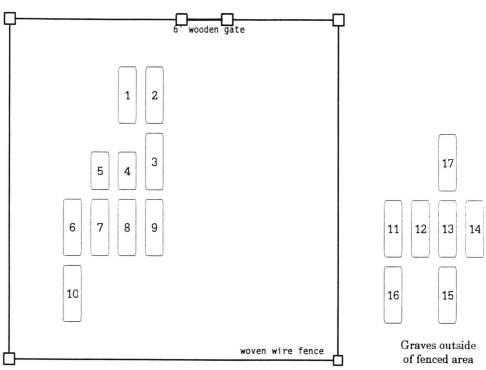

6' wooden gate

woven wire fence

Graves outside
of fenced area

* Drawn directly from Corps of Engineer Maps

Grave No.	Name of Interred	Reinterment Site
1	David T. Peters	Peterstown
2	Robert M. Peters	Peterstown
3	Samuel L. Anderson	Resthaven, Princeton
4	Paul J. Anderson	Resthaven, Princeton
5	J. G. Anderson, Jr.	Resthaven, Princeton
6	Mary E. Peters	Butler Cem., Tophet
7	Polly Ann Peters	Butler Cem., Tophet
8	James C. Peters	Butler Cem., Tophet
9	Edith R. Gore	Butler Cem., Tophet
10	Annie L. Ferguson	Resthaven, Princeton
11 - 17	Unknown	Peterstown

Military headstone of James Conrad Peters set at base of original headstone which was moved from Mercer Salt Works when graves were relocated.

family history explains that the look in James' eye was probably reminiscent of the look he had as he sighted down the barrel of his six-pound Napoleon fieldpiece at the Union forces at Fort Donelson. The husband did not attempt to interfere with the rescue mission, and James, his daughter and her children went home to Mercer Salt Works.

James' unfailing faith in God and his love of family stayed with him up to his last days. The deeds and exploits of James Conrad Peters live on through his diary that still exists and the rich history of this family that has endured.

Family gathering at the setting of headstone of James Conrad Peters at Peters-Anderson Cemetery at Mercer Salt Works in 1912. James' widow, Polly Ann is standing just to the left of the headstone. Author's collection

Appendix A:
Poems From the Diary

There are several beautiful poems scattered throughout the diary. We have not been able to determine exactly when these poems were written. Rather than scatter them throughout the narrative, we have assembled them here together. The last two poems, obviously written during the War, are especially touching. (Page numbers are actual diary page numbers.)

Page 2:

> *This world is like a friendship*
> *For man's illusion given*
> *The smiles of joy the tears of woe*
> *Deceitful shine deceitful glow*
> *There's nothing true but heaven's plane*
> *2 And false the light on glory*
> *As fading hues of even bloom*
> *And love and hope and beauty*
> *Are blossoms gathered for the tomb.*
> *There's nothing bright but heaven*
> *3 Poor wanderers of a stormy day*
> *From wave to wave we are driven*
> *And fancy flash and reason say*
> *Serve but to light the troubled way*
> *There's nothing calm but heaven.*
> > *James*

Page 37:

> *A friend in need is*
> *a friend indeed.*
> > *James C Peters*
> *This world is all a fleeting show*
> *Of a man's delusions given*
> *---------of by the tears of woe*
> *Beautiful show beautiful flow*
> *There's nothing true but heaven*
> > *Verity   James C Peters*
> > *December 5th 1858*
> > *Mercer County Va*

(This appears to be more of the poem from page 2 of the diary.)

Page 4:

Oh I have not loved
lightly I still think of
thee yet & I will love
thee until lifes sun
does set.
                    J C Peters

Page 5:

Remember me when clouds are bright
With glory flame unfurled
Remember me when dreary night
wraps up the slumbering world
When loudly howls the wintry blast
Through every forest tree
And memory lingers on the past.
Ah, then sweet love Remember me.
                    James C Peters
Remember me when far away
For I remember thee every day.
                    JCP

Page 42:

The Absent Soldier
My dear wife waits my coming
My child it lisps my name
The wild birds in the woods are singing
The wind blows over the plain
But I am far away from them
But I am coming to my home again
Though foes may thickly stand
Or shed my last drop of blood
Contending for my native land.
Oh Dixie Dixie
I will live & die for dixie
my sunny southern home.
Oh poor bleeding Dixie
Oh that I could help thee
* -------was over & cannot help thee*

Page 44:

This Confederate flag
Oh long may it wave
oer the land of the Free
and the home of the brave.

Celebration at Mercer Salt Works of golden wedding anniversary of James Conrad Peters and Polly Ann Thompson, Sept. 29, 1909. James and Polly Ann are seated in middle of front row of adults. Children and grandchildren are all in this photo. Author's collection

Appendix B
The Family of James and Polly Ann

James Conrad Peters and wife Polly Ann Thompson were the parents of ten children. We have listed here the basic facts about their children, and have also listed their grandchildren.

1. <u>Mary Elizabeth Peters</u>, born Sept. 13, 1860, died Feb. 2, 1917. Never married. Was postmistress at Mercer Salt Works P.O. between 1900 and 1914. Lived with her parents probably her whole life. Originally buried in Peters-Anderson Cemetery at the Salt Works. Remains later moved by Corps of Engineers to Butler Cemetery, near Tophet in Mercer Co., West Virginia.

2. <u>Sarah Emeline Peters</u>, born June 9, 1862 in Mercer County. Married William N. Dickinson May 24, 1882 in Mercer County. Known as "Mommie Peters." They were the great grandparents of the editor. William N. Dickinson born Oct. 4, 1855 in Giles Co., Virginia, died Aug. 29, 1915 in Mercer County. They were the parents of six children: Frank, born Apr. 18, 1883 who married Lelia Spangler (grandparents of the editor), Harry, born Jan. 9, 1885 and died in infancy, William M., born Oct. 4, 1887 who married first Minnie B. Thompson and second Lula B. Cooper, Lula, born Apr. 23, 1890 who married Kyle Farley, Ethel, born Feb. 9, 1893 who married Chafe Thompson, and Mettie, born Aug. 16, 1895 who married Loren Williams. Sarah E. died Mar. 12, 1929 of "infirmities of age." Buried Rest Haven Cemetery, Princeton, West Virginia within sight of Capt. Napoleon B. French's grave.

3. <u>John Henry Peters</u>, born Sept. 15, 1866 in Monroe County but probably near Mercer Salt Works. Married Martha Camden "Cammie" Walker Apr. 11, 1894. She was born Aug. 1, 1878. They were the parents of three children: James Walker, born Feb. 3, 1901, Charles William, born Oct. 7, 1903, and Carrie Sue, born Mar. 20, 1908. John Henry served as a policeman in Washington, DC for many years. Died Feb. 26, 1957 and buried with his parents at Butler Cemetery, Tophet, West Virginia.

4. <u>Mettie Burke Peters</u>, born Aug. 16, 1868 also in Monroe County. Married James David Anderson, Jr. on Nov. 26, 1890 at Mercer Salt Works. James worked for the C & O Railway Co. They were the parents of three children: Annie Laurie, born Sept. 21, 1892, James Morton, born Sept. 23, 1895, and Robert Henry, born Mar. 25, 1899 and died Aug. 13, 1899. Mettie died on Aug. 16, three days after the death of Robert Henry. Her obituary stated she died on the 15th of consumption at her father's house near Mercer Salt Works. James Conrad Peters and Polly took the two older children, Annie Laurie and James Morton, and raised them. These two children appear in the 1900 census of Summers County in the household with James Conrad and Polly. Mettie is buried in the J. D. Anderson Cemetery.

5. <u>Fannie Snidow Peters</u>, born Dec. 25, 1870 in Monroe County. Married Alonzo L. "Lonz" Butler on Oct. 29, 1890 in Mercer County. He was born Jan. 14, 1868. Lonz was president of the Summers County Court in 1940. He owned land in both Summers and Monroe Counties and raised cattle and sheep. They were the parents of seven children: Mamie Maude, born Aug. 5, 1891, William Bryan, born Sept. 16, 1896, Florence, born Mar. 7, 1898, Thomas Peters, born Mar. 26, 1901, Charles Snidow, born Dec. 26, 1904, James Alexander, born Mar. 13, 1909 and Dorothy born Jan. 20, 1914.

Fannie died Apr. 3, 1951 in the Hinton, West Virginia hospital and is buried in the Butler Cemetery with her parents. Her obituary stated that she had been in ill health for some time before entering the hospital.

6. <u>William Karnes Peters</u>, born Apr. 12, 1873 in Mercer County. Married Ida D. "Ide" Butler on Nov. 14, 1894. She was born Oct. 9, 1876. William K. was a merchant and farmer in Summers and Mercer Counties, operating the general store at Lick Creek for some years. They also owned a home in Princeton, West Virginia. They were the parents of five children: Christian, born Sept. 19, 1895, Mabel Clara, born Sept. 1, 1898, Edith Ruth, born Jan. 13, 1903, Fay Butler, born Sept. 18, 1905, and William Cary, born Aug. 25, 1908. William Karnes died at their home in Princeton on July 20, 1949.

7. <u>Unnamed female</u>, born Oct. 13, 1875 and died Oct. 15, 1875. Mercer County death records (Book I) show she was born and died in Mercer County. Not mentioned in the Peters family book by Okey E. Peters.

8. <u>Annie Laura Peters</u>, born Mar. 25, 1877. Married Jabez G. Anderson on Nov. 27, 1895 in Mercer County. They were the parents of seven children: Henry Carl, born Nov. 14, 1896, Samuel Luther, born Jan. 21, 1902, Zettie Mary, born Jan. 15, 1904, Myrtle Florence, born Feb. 2, 1907, William Edwin, born July 1, 1914, Paul James, born and died Dec. 12, 1918, Jabez Garland, Jr., born and died Dec. 11, 1920. Three of these children: Samuel L., Paul J., and Jabez G., Jr. were also buried originally in the Peters-Anderson Cemetery at Mercer Salt Works. Their graves were relocated to Rest Haven Cemetery at Princeton, West Virginia. Annie Laura died Aug. 1, 1951 and is also buried at Princeton.

9. <u>Edith Rebecca Peters</u>, born July 25, 1880. The Peters book says she was born at Glen Lyn in Giles County, Virginia. Married Thomas H. Gore on Mar. 4, 1903 at Athens in Mercer County. He was born Nov. 4, 1877. Supposedly Edith Rebecca did not attend school until after she was 16 years old, but did graduate from Hinton High School. Thomas Gore was a farmer and also worked in the mercantile business. He suffered from tuberculosis in later life. They were the parents of five children: Amy Edith, born Jan. 15, 1904, Robert Henry, born Dec. 13, 1905 and died seven months later, James Charles, born Mar. 5, 1908, Anna Ruth, born June 4, 1910, and Lucy Rebecca, born June 2, 1912. Edith Rebecca died Mar. 8, 1915 and was originally buried at Mercer Salt Works. Her grave was relocated to Butler Cemetery at Tophet beside her parents. Thomas Gore died in 1939 and is buried in the Fairview Cemetery at Narrows, Virginia.

10. <u>Lucy Jane Peters</u>, born Jan. 30, 1884 and died Jan. 8, 1889. No further data.

Abbreviations Used in the Notes
(See the Bibliography for complete entries.)

CV: Confederate Veteran Magazine
CSR: Compiled Service Records of Confederate Soldiers from Virginia
OR: Official Records of the Union and Confederate Armies
SHSP: Southern Historical Society Papers

Notes to Chapter I

1. National Archives, Revolutionary War Military and Pension Records, Christian Peters.
2. Okey Erwin Peters, *Conrad Peters and Wife Clara Snidow*, (Paducah, KY: Paducah Printing Co., 1940's), 160-163.
3. R. F. Fleshman, "History of Peterstown Community," (Morgantown, WV: Agricultural Extension Div., 1924), 2.
4. Peters, 155.
5. National Archives, *Seventh Census of the United States, 1850 Census of Virginia*, microfilm publication M653.
6. Peters, 150. This account is confirmed by some sources, although the official papers regarding the court case have disappeared from the Mercer County Courthouse at Princeton, WV.
7. Roane County, WV deed books, Roane County Courthouse, Spencer, WV.

Notes to Chapter II

1. Oren F. Morton, *A History of Preston County, West Virginia*, (Kingwood, WV: Journal Pub. Co., 1914), 139.
2. Elmer G. Dickinson, "The Influence of Sectionalism upon the History of the James River and Kanawha Company in Western Virginia" (Master's Thesis, Duke University, 1941), 33.
3. Henry Howe, *The Times of the Rebellion in the West*, (Cincinnati: Howe's Book Concern, 1867), 35.
4. National Archives, *Eighth Census of the United States, 1860 Census of Virginia*, microfilm publication M653.
5. *Ibid.*
6. *Ibid.*

Notes to Chapter III

1. Okey Erwin Peters, *Conrad Peters and Wife Clara Snidow*, (Paducah, KY: Paducah Printing Co., 1940's), 150.
2. *Ibid.*, 150.
3. National Archives, *Seventh Census of the United States, 1850 Census of Virginia*, microfilm publication M653.
4. *Holy Bible*, King James Version, 1715.
5. National Archives, *Eighth Census of the United States, 1860 Census of Virginia*, microfilm publication M653.
6. Peters, 151.

Notes to Chapter IV

1. David E. Johnston, *A History of Middle New River Settlements and Contiguous Territory*, Reprint, (Radford, VA: Commonwealth Press, 1969), 186.
2. S. Bassett French, "Biographical Sketches," microfilm, West Virginia Archives.
3. Michael West, *The Gauley, Mercer and Western Artillery*, (Lynchburg: H. E. Howard, 1991), 75.
4. OR, I, Vol. 51, Part 2, 245.
5. CSR, Record Group 109, microfilm, WV Archives.
6. Robert S. Lanier, editor, *The Photographic History of the Civil War: Armies & Leaders*, Reprint, (New

York: The Fairfax Press, 1983), 252.

7. West, 82.
8. *Ibid.*, 152.
9. Robert C. Wood, *Confederate Handbook*, reprint, (Falls Church, VA: Sterling Press, 1982), 22.
10. Lew Wallace, "The Capture of Fort Donelson," *Battles and Leaders of the Civil War*, vol. 1, (New York: the Century Co., 1887), 400.
11. Benjamin F. Cooling, "Forts Henry & Donelson," *Blue & Gray Magazine*, Feb. 1992, 11.
12. CSR, 30th Battalion, under the Record of Events for the unit is noted: "The company as Light Artillery left Dublin Depot Dec. 28, 1861, with 4 guns under orders for Bowling Green, Ky...."
13. West, 83.
14. Michael J. Pauley, *Unreconstructed Rebel, The Life of Gen. John McCausland C.S.A.*, (Charleston, WV: Pictorial Histories, 1993), 21.

Notes to Chapter V

1. Lee A. Wallace, Jr. *A Guide to Virginia Military Organizations 1861-1865*, Reprint. (Lynchburg, VA: H. E. Howard, 1986), 22.
2. P. Michael West, *The Gauley, Mercer and Western Artillery*, (Lynchburg, VA: H. E. Howard, 1991), 85.
3. Thomas E. Griess, editor, *Atlas for the American Civil War*, (Wayne, NJ: Avery Pub. Group, 1986), 4.
4. Lew Wallace, "The Capture of Fort Donelson," *Battles and Leaders of the Civil War*, vol. 1, (New York: The Century Co., 1887), 398.
5. CSR, 51st Virginia Infantry, WV Archives microfilm. (The 51st Virginia's other chaplain was Burton S. Highley, but according to his service records, he was not commissioned until April 1863 so the acting chaplain in early 1862 must have been Garland.)
6. *Holy Bible*, King James Version, 1715.
7. Stewart Sifakis, *Who Was Who in the Confederacy*, (New York: Facts on File, 1988), 119.
8. Elizabeth Shelby Kinkead, *A History of Kentucky*, (New York: American Book Co., 1896), 180.
9. D. B. Baldwin, 51st Va Infantry, quoted in *51st Virginia Infantry*, by James A. Davis, (Lynchburg, VA: H. E. Howard, 1984), 8.
10. West, 89.
11. James Hamilton, *The Battle of Fort Donelson*, (New York: A. S. Barnes, 1968), 33.
12. Benjamin F. Cooling, "Forts Henry & Donelson," *Blue & Gray Magazine*, Feb. 1992, 19.
13. West, 90.
14. Guy started his journal while in prison at Camp Chase, Ohio, two months after his capture at Ft. Donelson. He not only interviewed his comrades who were at Camp Chase with him, but he also tried to supplement his own memory with what newspaper articles he could obtain. While his entries are written two months after the fact, he still provides valuable information about the Battle of Fort Donelson.
15. Cooling, 19.
16. John Henry Guy, "A Virginian At Fort Donelson: Excerpts From the Prison Journal of John Henry Guy," *Tennessee Historical Quarterly*, Vol XXVII, 1968, 177.
17. CSR, "Record of Events" for Company B, 30th Battalion Virginia Sharpshooters (French's Battery after reorganization), microfilm.
18. Cooling, 20.
19. Hamilton, 84: stated that Floyd arrived together with his three batteries.
20. Guy, 178.
21. West, 92.
22. Cooling, 19.
23. Lew Wallace, 403.
24. Guy, 180.
25. Hamilton, 86 and West, 94.
26. Hamilton, 89.
27. Lew Wallace, 403 and Hamilton, 117.
28. Kinkead, 182.
29. Cooling, 46.
30. Hamilton, 113.

31. West, 95.
32. Guy, 179.
33. West, 98.
34. Hamilton, 116.
35. West, 96.
36. Hamilton, 192.
37. *Ibid.*, 264.
38. Cooling, 49.
39. Hamilton, 288.
40. *Ibid.*, 301.
41. Guy, 185.
42. OR, I, VII, 381.
43. Guy, 185.
44. OR, I, VII, 254.

Notes to Chapter VI

1. James Hamilton, *The Battle of Fort Donelson*, (New York: A. S. Barnes, 1968), 344.
2. CSR, "Record of Events" for Company B, 30th Battalion Virginia Sharpshooters (French's Battery after reorganization), microfilm.
3. John Henry Guy, "A Virginian At Fort Donelson: Excerpts From the Prison Journal of John Henry Guy," *Tennessee Historical Quarterly*, Vol XXVII, 1968, 186.
4. *Ibid.*, 188.
5. Comte de Paris, *History of the Civil War in America*, vol. 1, translated from the French, (Philadelphia: Porter & Coates, 1875), 485.
6. Stanley F. Horn, ed., *Tennessee's War 1861-1865*, (Nashville: Civil War Centennial Comm., 1965), 52.
7. OR, I, VII, 271.
8. B. Franklin Cooling, "John B. Floyd," *Encyclopedia of the Confederacy*, vol. 2, (New York: Simon & Schuster, 1993), 593.
9. CV, XV, (1907), 234.
10. *Ibid.*, 234.
11. "Confederate Soldiers, Sailors & Civilians Who Died as Prisoners of War at Camp Douglas, Chicago, IL 1862-65," (Kalamazoo, MI: Edgar Gray Publications, n.d.), intro.
12. George Levy, *To Die in Chicago, Confederate Prisoners at Camp Douglas*, (Evanston, IL: Evanston Publishing, 1994), 39.
13. *Ibid.*, 37.
14. *Ibid.*, 156.
15. *Ibid.*, 57.
16. Okey Erwin Peters, *Conrad Peters and Wife Clara Snidow*, (Paducah, KY: Paducah Printing Co., 1940's), 152.
17. Levy, 72.
18. CSR, 30th Battalion Va. Sharpshooters, microfilm.
19. *Ibid.*, 74.
20. *Ibid.*, 81.
21. J. G. Randall and David H. Donald, *The Civil War and Reconstruction*, (Lexington, MA: D. C. Heath, 1969), 334.
22. CSR, 30th Battalion Va. Sharpshooters, microfilm.
23. P. Michael West, *The Gauley, Mercer and Western Artillery*, (Lynchburg, VA: H. E. Howard, 1991), 105.

Notes to Chapter VII

1. CSR, Company B, 30th Battalion Virginia Sharpshooters (French's Battery after reorganization), microfilm.
2. Frederick Way, Jr., *Way's Packet Directory 1848-1983*, (Athens, OH: Ohio University, 1983), also C. Bradford Mitchell, ed., *Merchant Steam Vessels of the United States 1790-1868*, (Staten Island, NY: Steamship Historical Society of America, 1975).

3. Henry Walke, "The Western Flotilla at Fort Donelson, Island Number Ten, Fort Pillow and Memphis," *Battles and Leaders of the Civil War*, vol. 1, (New York: The Century Co., 1887), 438.

4. Thomas L. Connelly, *Civil War Tennessee, Battles and Leaders*, (Knoxville, University of Tenn. Press, 1994), 51.

5. *Ibid.*, 30.

6. CSR, 30th Battalion, microfilm.

7. William C. Davis, ed. *The Guns of 1862*, vol. II of *The Image of War 1861-1865*, (Garden City, NY: Doubleday & Co., 1982), 277.

8. Richard N. Current, ed., *Encyclopedia of the Confederacy*, vol 3, (New York: Simon & Schuster, 1993), 1059.

9. Thomas E. Gries, ed., *Atlas for the American Civil War*, (Wayne, NJ: Avery Pub. Group, 1986), plate 2.

10. Current, vol. 3, 1330.

11. CSR, 30th Battalion, microfilm.

Notes to Chapter VIII

1. CSR, 30th Battalion Sharpshooters "Record of Events," microfilm.

2. "Civil War Diary of John Schowen," *The History of Putnam County*, (WV) William D. Wintz, ed., Upper Vandalia Hist. Society, Oct. 1984 and Jan. 1985 volumes.

3. Jack L. Dickinson, *8th Virginia Cavalry*, 2nd edition, (Lynchburg,VA: H. E. Howard, 1986), 42.

4. Oliver P. Temple, *East Tennessee and the Civil War*, reprint, (Johnson City, TN: Overmountain Press, 1995), 492.

5. Terry Lowry, *26th Battalion Virginia Infantry*, (Lynchburg,VA: H. E. Howard, 1991), 37.

6. Roger U. Delauter, Jr., *62nd Virginia Infantry*, (Lynchburg,VA: H. E. Howard, 1988), 30.

7. Thomas A. Lewis, *The Shenandoah in Flames*, (Alexandria,VA: Time Life Books, 1987), 34.

8. Schowen diary, 7.

9. Edward Raymond Turner, *The New Market Campaign (1864)*, (Richmond: Whittet & Shepperson, 1912), 130-131.

10. James C. Holland, *Shenandoah Valley Memories of the War Between the States*, (York, PA: York Graphic Services, 1992), 106.

11. CSR, 30th Battalion, microfilm.

12. William C. Davis, *The Battle of New Market*, (Baton Rouge: LA State Univ. Press, 1975), 195.

13. James H. Mays, *Four Years for Old Virginia*, (Los Angeles: Swordsman Pub, 1970), 36.

14. Jed. Hotchkiss, *Virginia*, vol. III of *Confederate Military History*, (Blue & Gray Press), 469.

15. Delauter, 128.

16. J. G. Randall and David H. Donald, *The Civil War and Reconstruction*, 2nd ed., (Lexington, MA: D. C. Heath, 1969), 420.

17. CSR, 30th Battalion, microfilm.

18. Schowen diary, 5.

19. Lowry, 53.

20. Schowen diary, also Douglas S. Freeman, *Lee's Lieutenants*, vol. III, 563, says the other divisions (other than Gordon's) "joined in the chase."

21. OR, I, 42, part 2, 861.

22. Glenn. H. Worthington, *Fighting For Time*, reprint, (Shippensburg, PA: Beidel Printing House, 1985), 208.

23. George E. Pond, *The Shenandoah Valley in 1864*, (New York: Charles Scribner's Sons, 1892), 154.

24. Schowen diary, 6.

25. Pond, 165.

26. Jeffry D. Wert, *From Winchester to Cedar Creek*, (New York: Simon & Schuster, 1987), 92.

27. Schowen diary, 6.

28. OR, I, 43, part 2, 146.

29. OR, I, 43, part 2, 110.

30. OR, I, 43, part 1, 554.

Notes to Chapter IX

1. Quoted in SHSP, Vol. 18, 114.
2. CSR, 30th Battalion Sharpshooters, records of James Conrad Peters.
3. Edwin W. Beitzell, *Point Lookout Prison Camp for Confederates*, (Berryville,Va: Virginia Book Co., 1972), 61.
4. *Ibid.*, 97.
5. CV, XXXIV, 52.
6. *Ibid.*, 61.
7. Rev. J. B. Traywick, "Prison Life at Point Lookout," SHSP, Vol. 18, 432.
8. James I. Robertson, Jr., *Soldiers Blue & Gray*, (New York: Warner Books, 1988). Also CV, XXI, 55 and 524.
9. OR, II, 8, 133.
10. CV, XVIII, 472.
11. OR, II, 8, 1001, returns for Point Lookout prison give the peak number of prisoners as 20,110 for April, 1865. Also Richard N. Current, ed., *Encyclopedia of the Confederacy*, Vol 3, (New York: Simon & Schuster, 1993), 1221.
12. "List Showing inscription on monument to Confederate soldiers and sailors who died at Point Lookout," TS at West Virginia Archives and History, N.P, N.D. Also CSR, 30th Battalion Sharpshooters.
13. Traywick, 431.

Notes to Chapter X

1. CSR, 30th Battalion, records of James Conrad Peters.
2. H. M. Calhoun, *Twixt North and South,* (Franklin, WV: McCoy Pub., 1974), xvii.

Notes to Chapter XI

1. J. G. Randall and David H. Donald, *The Civil War and Reconstruction,* 2nd ed., (Lexington, MA: D. C. Heath, 1969), 547.
2. Summers Co. Historical Society, *The History of Summers County West Virginia 1984,*(Marceline, MO: Walsworth Press, 1984),49.
3. *Ibid.*, 49.
4. Charles Henry Ambler, *West Virginia The Mountain State*, (New York: Prentice-Hall, 1940), 255.
5. Mercer County Historical Society, *Mercer County History 1984*, (Marceline, MO: Walsworth Press, 1985),116.
6. James H. Miller, *History of Summers County*, (Hinton,WV: np, 1908), 206.
7. Kyle McCormick, *The Story of Mercer County*, (Charleston,WV: Charleston Printing, 1957), 31.
8. National Archives, *Tenth Census of the United States, 1880 Census of West Virginia,*microfilm publication M653.
9. National Archives, *Twelfth Census of the United States, 1900 Census of West Virginia*, microfilm publication M653.
10. Summers County Deed Books, Hinton,WV.
11. Miller, 505.
12. U.S. Army Corps of Engineers "Cemetery Relocation General Data Sheet, Peters-Anderson Cemetery," 1953.
13. U.S. Army Corps of Engineers maps, "New River Bluestone Reservoir Project, Cemetery Relocation Disinterment and Reinterment Cemeteries," 1953.
14. U.S. Army Corps of Engineers "Cemetery Relocation General Data Sheet, Peters-Anderson Cemetery," 1953.

Bibliography

BOOKS AND PAMPHLETS

Ambler, Charles Henry. *West Virginia The Mountain State.* New York: Prentice-Hall, 1940.

Beitzell, Edwin W. *Point Lookout Prison Camp for Confederates.* Berryville,VA: Virginia Book Co., 1972.

Calhoun, H. M. *Twixt North and South.* Franklin,WV: McCoy Pub. Co., 1974.

Clarke, H. C., ed. *The Confederate States Almanac, and Repository of Useful Knowledge, for 1862.* 1862. Reprint. Summerville, GA: Brannon Pub. Co.

Comte de Paris. *History of the Civil War in America.* (Translated from the French.) Philadelphia: Porter & Coates, 1875.

Connelly, Thomas L. *Civil War Tennessee, Battles and Leaders.* Knoxville,TN: University of Tennessee Press, 1994.

Cooling, Benjamin Franklin. *Forts Henry and Donelson: The Key to the Confederate Heartland.* Knoxville,TN: University of Tennessee Press, 1987.

Cummings, Charles M. *Yankee Quaker Confederate General, The Curious Career of Bushrod Rust Johnson.* Reprint. Columbus, OH: The General's Books, 1993.

Current, Richard N., ed. in chief. *Encyclopedia of the Confederacy.* 4 vols. New York: Simon & Schuster, 1993.

Davis, James A. *51st Virginia Infantry.* Lynchburg,VA: H. E. Howard, 1984.

Davis, William C., ed. *The Guns of '62.* Volume 2 of *The Image of War: 1861-1865.* Garden City, NY: Doubleday & Co., 1982.

Delauter, Roger U., Jr. *62nd Virginia Infantry.* Lynchburg,VA: H. E. Howard, 1988.

Dickinson, Jack L. *Tattered Uniforms and Bright Bayonets, West Virginia's Confederate Soldiers.* Huntington,WV: Marshall University Foundation, 1995.

_____.*8th Virginia Cavalry.* 2nd edition, Lynchburg,VA: H. E. Howard, 1986.

Early, Lt. Gen. Jubal A. *A Memoir of the Last Year of the War For Independence in the Confederate States of America.* Lynchburg: Charles W. Button, 1867.

Foote, Shelby. *The Civil War: A Narrative.* Volume 1. New York: Random House, 1958.

Freeman, Douglas Southall. *Lee's Lieutenants.* 3 volumes. New York: Charles Scribner's Sons, 1944.

Gallagher, Gary W., ed. *Struggle for the Shenandoah.* Kent, OH: Kent State Univ. Press., 1991.

Gordon, John B. *Confederate Handbook.* Reprint. Falls Church,VA: Sterling Press, 1982.

Griess, Thomas E., ed. *Atlas for The American Civil War.* Wayne, NJ: Avery Publishing Group, 1986.

Hamilton, James. *The Battle of Fort Donelson.* New York: A. S. Barnes & Co., 1968.

Hogg, Ian V. *Weapons of the Civil War.* New York: The Military Press, 1987.

Holland, James C. *Shenandoah Valley Memories of the War Between the States.* York, PA: York Graphic Services, 1992.

Horn, Stanley F., ed. *Tennessee's War 1861-1865.* Nashville: Tennessee Civil War Centennial Committee, 1965.

Hotchkiss, Maj. Jed. *Virginia.* Volume 3 of *Confederate Military History,* Reprint, Blue and Gray Press, N.D.

Howe, Henry. *The Times of the Rebellion in the West.* Cincinnati: Howe's Book Concern, 1867.

Hughes, Nathaniel Cheairs and Roy P. Stonesifer, Jr. *The Life and Wars of Gideon J. Pillow.* Chapel Hill: The University of North Carolina Press, 1993.

Johnson, R. R. and C. C. Buel, editors. *Battles and Leaders of the Civil War.* 4 vols. New York: The Century Co., 1887.

Johnston, David E. *A History of Middle New River Settlements.* 1906. Reprint. Radford,VA: Commonwealth Press, 1969.

Kinkead, Elizabeth Shelby. *A History of Kentucky.* New York: American Book Co., 1896.

Lanier, Robert S., ed. *The Photographic History of the Civil War: Armies & Leaders.* Reprint. New York: Fairfax Press, 1983.

Levy, George. *To Die in Chicago: Confederate Prisoners at Camp Douglas.* Evanston, IL: Evanston Publishing, 1994.

Lewis, Thomas A. *The Shenandoah in Flames.* Alexandria, VA: Time-Life Books, 1987.

Lowry, Terry. *26th Battalion Virginia Infantry.* Lynchburg, VA: H. E. Howard, 1991.

Mays, James H. *Four Years for Old Virginia.* Los Angeles, CA: Swordsman Pub., 1970.

McCormick, Kyle. *The Story of Mercer County*. Charleston,WV: Charleston Printing Co., 1957.

Mercer County Hist. Society. *Mercer County History 1984*. Marceline, MO: Walsworth Press, 1985.

Miller, James H. *History of Summers County*. Hinton,WV: n.p. 1908.

Morton, Oren F. *A History of Preston County West Virginia*. Kingwood,WV: Journal Pub. Co., 1914.

Pauley, Michael J. *Unreconstructed Rebel, The Life of Gen. John McCausland C.S.A.* Charleston,WV: Pictorial Histories Pub. Co., 1993.

Peters, Okey E. *Conrad Peters and Wife Clara Snidow Their Descendants and Their Ancestry*. Paducah, KY: Paducah Printing Co., 1940's.

Randall, J. G. and David H. Donald. *The Civil War and Reconstruction*. Lexington, MA: D.C. Heath, 1969.

Robertson, James I., Jr. *Soldiers Blue & Gray*. New York: Warner Books, 1988.

Scott, J. L. *36th Virginia Infantry*. Lynchburg,VA: H. E. Howard, 1987.

Sifakis, Stewart. *Compendium of the Confederate Armies: Virginia*. New York: Facts on File, 1992.

_____*Who Was Who in the Confederacy*. New York: Facts on File, 1988.

Stern, Philip Van Doren. *The Confederate Navy, A Pictorial History*. New York: Bonanza Books, 1962.

Stickles, Arndt M. *Simon Bolivar Buckner*. Chapel Hill: University of North Carolina Press, 1940.

Summers Co. Historical Society. *The History of Summers County West Virginia 1984*. Marceline, MO: Waslworth Press, 1984.

Symonds, Craig L. *A Battlefield Atlas of the Civil War*. 2nd ed. Baltimore: The Nautical and Aviation Pub. Co., 1983.

Temple, Oliver P. *East Tennessee and the Civil War*. Reprint. Johnson City,TN: Overmountain Press, 1995.

United States War Department. *War of the Rebellion: A Compilation of the Official Records of the Union and Confederate Armies*. 128 vols. Washington, DC: Government Printing Office, 1880-1901.

Vineyard, T. E. *Battles of the Civil War*. Spencer, WV: n.p., 1914.

Wallace, Lee A., Jr. *A Guide to Virginia Military Organizations 1861-1865*. Reprint. Lynchburg,VA: H. E. Howard, 1986.

Wert, Jeffry D. *From Winchester to Cedar Creek: The Shenandoah Campaign of 1864*. New York: Simon & Schuster, 1989.

West, Michael. *The Gauley, Mercer and Western Artillery*. Lynchburg,Va: H. E. Howard, Inc., 1991.

Worthington, Glenn H. *Fighting For Time*. Reprint. Shippensburg, PA: Beidel Printing House, 1985.

MAGAZINES AND JOURNALS

Cooling, Benjamin F. "Forts Henry and Donelson Union Victory on the Twin Rivers." *Blue & Gray Magazine*, Feb. 1992.

_____. "Virginians and West Virginians at Fort Donelson, Feb. 1862." *West Virginia History Quarterly*, Vol XXVIII, Oct. 1966, No. 1.

Confederate Veteran, Nashville, 1896-1907.

"Civil War Diary of John Schowen," *The History of Putnam County*, William D. Wintz, ed., Upper Vandalia Hist. Society, Oct. 1984 and Jan. 1985 volumes.

Guy, John Henry. "A Virginian at Fort Donelson: Excerpts From the Prison Journal of John Henry Guy." *Tennessee Historical Quarterly*, Vol XXVII, 1968.

Long, David E. "Cover-up at Cold Harbor." *Civil War Times Illustrated*, June, 1977.

Thomas, Gary and Richard Andrew, "Houses of Misery and Hope," *Civil War*, Issue 59, Dec. 1996.

Traywick, Rev. J. B. "Prison Life at Point Lookout." *Southern Historical Society Papers*, Richmond: Southern Historical Society, 1890.

Walker, Peter Franklin. "Command Failure: The Fall of Forts Henry and Donelson." *Tennessee Historical Quarterly*, Dec. 1957.

MANUSCRIPTS

Dickinson, Elmer G. "The Influence of Sectionalism upon the History of the James River and Kanawha Company in Western Virginia." Master's Thesis, Duke University, 1941.

Dickinson, Jack L. *The Civil War Diary of James Conrad Peters, Sgt., Company 'B' 30th Battalion Va. Sharpshooters CSA*. MS. Privately published, 1990.

Edgar Gray Publications. "Confederate Soldiers, Sailors & Civilians Who Died as Prisoners of War at

Camp Douglas, Chicago, Ill." Kalamazoo, MI: Edgar Gray Pubs., n.d.

Fleshman, R. F. "History of Peterstown Community." TS. Morgantown, WV: Agricultural Extension Div., 1924.

NEWSPAPERS

Hinton, WV, *Independent Herald*, Jan. 12, 1911.

New York, *Harper's Weekly*, Sat., Mar. 15, 1862.

Union, WV, *Monroe Watchman*.

MISCELLANEOUS SOURCES

Diary of James Conrad Peters, in possession of Henry Anderson, Mullens, WV.

French, S. Bassett. Biographical Sketches. Microfilm. West Virginia Archives.

"List showing inscription on monument to Confederate Soldiers and Sailors who died at Pt. Lookout," TS at West Virginia Archives, N.P., N.D.

Mercer County Courthouse, Princeton, WV: *Death Register (I)*.

National Archives. Eighth, Tenth and Twelfth Census of the United States, Microfilm publication M653.

U. S. Army Corps of Engineers, Huntington District, "New River-Bluestone Reservoir Project" Records.

Index

The three major subjects of this book: James Conrad Peters, French's Battery Virginia Artillery and 30th Battalion Virginia Sharpshooters do not appear in this index.

Peters, Mary Elizabeth-3, 14, 21, 82, 121, 128, 138
Peters, Mettie Burke-127, 138
Peters, Nancy-1
Peters, Nancy E.-3
Peters, Okey E.-139
Peters, Rebecca Jane-3, 14
Peters, Rhoda-1
Peters, Robert McNutt-128
Peters, Sarah (Sally)-1
Peters, Sarah Burke-3
Peters, Sarah Emeline-59, 82, 138
Peters, William Cary-139
Peters, William Karnes-139
Peters-Anderson Cemetery-128, 138-39
Petersburg, VA-79
Peterstown Cemetery-1, 128
Peterstown, WV-1, 3, 9-10, 85, 120, 128
Phillips, Squire-14
Pillow, Brig. Gen. Gideon J.-33, 35, 44, 46-47, 50
Pinch Gut (Creek)-12
Pittsburgh, PA-5
Polka (Poca) River-12
Pollard, AL-77
Port Republic, VA-105
Potomac River-96, 109
Princeton & Red Sulphur Road-119
Princeton, WV-16-17, 19, 85, 128, 138-39
Pt. Lookout, MD (prison)-54, 109-117
Pt. Pleasant, WV-8
Pulaski County, VA-20, 82, 90

Quinn, Mr.-12

Raleigh County, WV-12
Ramseur's Division-98-99
Red Sulphur Springs, WV-120
Reed, Thomas-24
Resthaven Cemetery-16, 128, 138-39
RF & P RR-79
Richmond & Danville RR-79
Richmond & Petersburg RR-79
Richmond & York River RR-79
Richmond, VA-5, 17, 19, 50, 77, 79, 82, 95
Roane County, WV-3, 13, 86
Rock Creek-12
Rockingham County, VA-1
Rodes, Gen. Robert-98, 102-04
Rodgers, A.-13

Rogersville, TN-88
Rose, T.-13
Ross, Pvt. William T.-111
Ross, Sgt. Samuel-62
Rosser's Brigade-105
Round Knob Cemetery-3
Round Knob Creek-3
Rudes Hill-105
Russell, Gen. D. A.-102
Russell, James H.-24
Russell, William-24
Russellville, KY-30-33

Salem, VA-95
Saltville, VA-86-87
Sarver, Henry-24
Sarver, John-24, 63
Schowen, Sgt. Maj. John M.-86, 88, 90, 93, 96, 98, 102
Shanklin's Ferry, WV-119
Shannon, John R.-24
Sharpsburg, MD-96
Shepherdstown, WV-96, 98
Sheridan, Gen. Phil-93, 98-99, 103-05
Shipp, Col. Scott-91
Shousetown, PA-65
Shrewsbury, Wm.-13
Shumaker, John J.-24
Shumate (family)-3, 9, 121
Shumate, Anderson-120, 127
Shumate, Ballard P.-127
Sigel, Gen. Franz-90-91
Sink Hole Mill, TN-30
Sinnett, Samuel-3, 86
Slab Fork-3
Smith's Brigade-96
Smith, Ben-11-13
Smith, Gen. Charles R.-24, 46
Smith, Daniel L.-24
Smith, Isaac A.-24
Smith, John W.-24
Smith, Joseph T.-24
Smith, Theodore, Jr.-24, 63
Smith, Brig. Gen. Thomas-96
Smithland, KY-51
Smyth County, VA-22
Snidow, Clara-1
Southern RR-76
Sower, John-24
Spangler, Florence B.-128
Spangler, Lelia-138
Spencer, WV-3, 86
St. Louis, MO-51-52, 54, 67
St. Mary's County, MD-109

Staley, Isaac-11
Stamp's Battery-86

Staunton, VA-87, 90, 93
Steele, William French-24, 62
Stephenson's Depot-98, 103
Stevenson, AL-26
Strasburg, VA-96
Summers County, WV-3, 9, 119, 127, 138-39
Symms, B. L.-60
Symms, Bettie-61

Tanner, Frederick-24
Tennessee Infantry, 3rd-54
Tennessee River-20, 67
Tensas Station-77
Tensaw River-77
Thomas, Boston W.-24
Thomas, Franklin M.-62
Thomas, George P.-24
Thomas, Green-24
Thomas, Henderson F.-24
Thomas, James H.-24, 63
Thomas, Lampkin Mckinney-24
Thompson, Andrew J.-14
Thompson, Chafe-138
Thompson, John-11
Thompson, Minnie B.-138
Thompson, Polly Ann-14, 31, 59, 82, 127-28, 138
Thompson, Sally-13
Thompson, William Henderson-14
Thornton, Andrew J.-24
Thornton, James A.-24, 63
Thornton, Thomas P.-24, 63, 69
Tilghman, Brig. Gen. Lloyd-32
Tiller, Hiram-24
Tiller, Thomas J.-24
Tiller, William A.-24
Tophet, WV-128, 138-39
Torbert, Gen. A. T.-99, 103, 105
Tracy, Edward George-24
Tracy, Harvey S.-24
Tracy, Roland-24, 63
Traywick, Rev. J. B.-110, 112, 114
Tredegar Iron Works-79
Truman, Thomas-13
Tucker, Col. Joseph H.-60-61, 63
Turner, Robert B.-24, 63
Tuttle, Rev. Edmund-55

Union, TN-22, 25
Union, WV-1
Universe-65, 67
Upperville, VA-96

Upton, Gen. Emory-102

Back Cover: County Map of Virginia and West Virginia by S. Augustus Mitchell and one of the first maps to show the new state of West Virginia. Probably printed between June 1863 and January 1864. Courtesy Special Collections Dept., University of Virginia Library